# TIMED READINGS PLUS

25 Two-Part Lessons
with Questions for
Building Reading Speed and Comprehension

### BOOK SEVEN

*Edward Spargo*

JAMESTOWN PUBLISHERS

*a division of* NTC/CONTEMPORARY PUBLISHING COMPANY
Lincolnwood, Illinois USA

**Timed Readings Plus, Book Seven, Level J**
Selection text adapted from Compton's Encyclopedia.
Used with permission of Compton's Learning Company.

ISBN: 0-89061-909-3

Published by Jamestown Publishers,
a division of NTC/Contemporary Publishing Group, Inc.,
4255 West Touhy Avenue,
Lincolnwood, Illinois, 60646 U.S.A.
©1998 by NTC/Contemporary Publishing Group, Inc.
All rights reserved. No part of this publication may be reproduced,
stored in a retrieval system, or transmitted in any form or by any means
electronic, mechanical, photocopying, recording, or otherwise,
without prior written permission of the Publisher.
Manufactured in the United States of America.

890 ML 0987654321

If students keep track of their own reading times, have them write the times at which they start and finish reading on a separate piece of paper and then figure and record their reading time as above.

Students should now answer the ten questions that follow the Part A selection. Responses are recorded by putting an X in the box next to the student's choice of answer. Correct responses to eight or more questions indicates satisfactory comprehension and recall.

## Teaching a Lesson: Part B

When students have finished Part A, they can move on to read the Part B selection. Although brief, these selections deliver all the content needed to attack the range of comprehension questions that follow.

Students next answer the comprehension questions that follow the Part B selection. Directions for answering the questions are provided with each question. Correct responses require deliberation and discrimination.

## Correcting and Scoring Answers

Using the Answer Key at the back of the book, students self-score their responses to the questions in Parts A and B. Incorrect answers should be circled and the correct answers should be marked. The number of correct answers for Part A and for Part B and the total correct answers should be tallied on the final page of the lesson.

## Using the Graphs

Reading times are plotted on the Reading Rate graph at the back of the book. The legend on the graph automatically converts reading times to words-per-minute rates. Comprehension totals are plotted on the Comprehension Scores graph. Plotting automatically converts the raw scores to a comprehension percentage based on four points per correct answer.

## Diagnosis and Evaluation

The Comprehension Skills Profile graph at the back of the book tracks student responses to the Part B comprehension questions. For each incorrect response, students should mark an X in the corresponding box on the graph. A column of Xs rising above other columns indicates a specific comprehension weakness. Using the profile, you can assess trends in student performance and suggest remedial work if necessary.

A student who has reached a peak in reading speed (with satisfactory comprehension) is ready to advance to the next book in the series. Before moving on to the next book, students should be encouraged to maintain their speed and comprehension on a number of lessons in order to consolidate their achievement.

# How to Use This Book

## Getting Started

**Study Part A: Reading Faster and Better.** Read and learn the steps to follow and the techniques to use to help you read more quickly and more efficiently.

**Study Part B: Mastering Reading Comprehension.** Learn what the five categories of comprehension are all about. Knowing what kind of comprehension response is expected from you and how to achieve that response will help you better comprehend all you read.

## Working a Lesson

**Find the Starting Lesson.** Locate the timed selection in Part A of the lesson that you are going to read. Wait for your instructor's signal to preview the selection. Your instructor will allow you 15 seconds for previewing.

**Read the Part A Selection.** When your instructor gives you the signal, begin reading. Read at a faster-than-normal speed. Read carefully so that you will be able to answer questions about what you have read.

**Record Your Reading Time.** When you finish reading, look at the blackboard and note your reading time. Write this time at the bottom of the page on the line labeled Reading Time.

**Answer the Part A Questions.** Answer the 10 questions that follow the selection. There are 5 fact questions and 5 thought questions. Choose the best answer to each question and put an X in that box.

**Read the Part B Selection.** This passage is less textbook-like and more story-like than the timed selection. Read well enough so that you can answer the questions that follow.

**Answer the Part B Questions.** These questions are different from traditional multiple-choice questions. In answering these questions, you must make three choices for each question. Instructions for answering each category of question are given. There are 15 responses for you to record.

**Correct Your Answers.** Use the Answer Key at the back of the book. For the Part A questions, circle any wrong answer and put an X in the box you should have marked. For the Part B questions, circle any wrong answer and write the correct letter or number next to it.

# Scoring Your Work

**Total Your Correct Answers.** Count your correct answers for Part A and for Part B. Record those numbers on the appropriate lines at the end of the lesson. Then add the two scores to determine your total correct answers. Record that number on the appropriate line.

# Plotting Your Progress

**Plot Your Reading Time.** Refer to the Reading Rate graph on page 116. On the vertical line that represents your lesson, put an X at the point where it intersects your reading time, shown along the left-hand side. The right-hand side of the graph will reveal your words-per-minute reading speed. Your instructor will review this graph from time to time to evaluate your progress.

**Plot Your Comprehension Scores.** Record your comprehension scores on the graph on page 117. On the vertical line that represents your lesson, put an X at the point where it intersects your total correct answers, shown along the left-hand side. The right-hand side of the graph will reveal your comprehension percentage. Your instructor will want to review this graph, too. Your achievement, as shown on both graphs, will determine your readiness to move on to higher and more challenging levels.

**Plot Your Comprehension Skills.** You will find the Comprehension Skills Profile on page 118. It is used to record your wrong answers only for the Part B questions. The five categories of questions are listed along the bottom. There are five columns of boxes, one column for each question. For every wrong answer, put an X in a box for that question. Your instructor will use this graph to detect any comprehension problems you may be experiencing.

# PART A: READING FASTER AND BETTER

## Step 1: Preview

When you read, do you start in with the first word, or do you look over the whole selection for a moment? Good readers preview the selection first. This helps make them good—and fast—readers. Here are the steps to follow when previewing the timed selection in Part A of each unit.

**1. Read the Title.** Titles are designed not only to announce the subject, but also to make the reader think. What can you learn from the title? What thoughts does it bring to mind? What do you already know about this subject?

**2. Read the First Sentence.** Read the first two sentences if they are short. The opening sentence is the writer's opportunity to greet the reader. Some writers announce what they hope to tell you in the selection. Some writers tell you why they are writing. Other writers just try to get your attention.

**3. Read the Last Sentence.** Read the final two sentences if they are short. The closing sentence is the writer's last chance to talk to you. Some writers repeat the main idea once more. Some writers draw a conclusion—this is what they have been leading up to. Other writers summarize their thoughts; they tie all the facts together.

**4. Scan the Selection.** Glance through the selection quickly to see what else you can pick up. Look for anything that can help you read the selection. Are there names, dates, or numbers? If so, you may have to read more slowly. Is the selection informative—containing a lot of facts, or is it conversational—an informal discussion with the reader?

## Step 2: Read for Meaning

When you read, do you just see words? Are you so occupied reading words that you sometimes fail to get the meaning? Good readers see beyond the words—they seek the meaning. This makes them faster readers.

**1. Build Concentration.** You cannot read with understanding if you are not concentrating. When you discover that your thoughts are straying, correct the situation right away. Avoid distractions and distracting situations. Keep the preview information in mind. This will help focus your attention on the selection.

**2. Read in Thought Groups.** A reader should strive to see words in meaningful combinations. If you see only a word at a time (called word-by-word reading), your comprehension suffers along with your speed.

**3. Question the Writer.** To sustain the pace you have set for yourself, and to maintain a high level of concentration and comprehension, question the writer as you read. Ask yourself such questions as, "What does this mean? How can I use this information?"

## Step 3: Grasp Paragraph Sense

The paragraph is the basic unit of meaning. If you can discover quickly and understand the main point of each paragraph, you can comprehend the writer's message. Good readers know how to find the main ideas quickly. This helps make them faster readers.

**1. Find the Topic Sentence.** The topic sentence, which contains the main idea, is often the first sentence of a paragraph. It is followed by sentences that support, develop, or explain the main idea. Sometimes a topic sentence comes at the end of a paragraph. When it does, the supporting details come first, building the base for the topic sentence. Some paragraphs do not have a topic sentence; all of the sentences combine to create a meaningful idea.

**2. Understand Paragraph Structure.** Every well-written paragraph has a purpose. The purpose may be to inform, define, explain, illustrate, and so on. The purpose should always relate to the main idea and expand on it. As you read each paragraph, see how the body of the paragraph is used to tell you more about the main idea.

## Step 4: Organize Facts

When you read, do you tend to see a lot of facts without any apparent connection or relationship? Understanding how the facts all fit together to deliver the writer's message is, after all, the reason for reading. Good readers organize facts as they read. This helps them read rapidly and well.

**1. Discover the Writer's Plan.** Every writer has a plan or outline to follow. If you can discover the writer's method of organization, you have a key to understanding the message. Sometimes the writer gives you obvious signals. The statement, "There are three reasons . . .," should prompt you to look for a listing of the three items. Other less obvious signal words such as *moreover, otherwise,* and *consequently* tell you the direction the writer is taking in delivering a message.

**2. Relate as You Read.** As you read the selection, keep the information learned during the preview in mind. See how the writer is attempting to piece together a meaningful message. As you discover the relationship among the ideas, the message comes through quickly and clearly.

# PART B: MASTERING READING COMPREHENSION

## Recognizing Words in Context

Always check to see if the words around a new word—its context—can give you some clue to its meaning. A word generally appears in a context related to its meaning. If the words *soil* and *seeds* appear in an article about gardens, for example, you can assume they are related to the topic of gardens.

Suppose you are unsure of the meaning of the word *expired* in the following paragraph:

> Vera wanted to take a book out, but her library card had expired.
> She had to borrow mine because she didn't have time to renew hers.

You could begin to figure out the meaning of *expired* by asking yourself, "What could have happened to Vera's library card that would make her have to borrow someone else's card?" You might realize that if she had to renew her card, it must have come to an end or run out. This would lead you to conclude that the word *expired* must mean to come to an end or run out. You would be right. The context suggested the meaning to you.

Context can also affect the meaning of a word you know. The word *key,* for instance, has many meanings. There are musical keys, door keys, and keys to solving a mystery. The context in which *key* occurs will tell you which meaning is right.

Sometimes a hard word will be explained by the words that immediately follow it. The word *grave* in the following sentence might give you trouble:

> He looked grave; there wasn't a trace of a smile on his lips.

You can figure out that the second part of the sentence explains the word *grave:* "wasn't a trace of a smile" indicates a serious look, so *grave* must mean serious.

The subject of a sentence and your knowledge about that subject might also help you determine the meaning of an unknown word. Try to decide the meaning of the word *revive* in the following sentence:

> Sunshine and water will revive those drooping plants.

The sentence is about giving plants light and water. You may know that plants need light and water to be healthy. If you know that drooping plants are not healthy, you can figure out that *revive* means to bring back to health.

# Distinguishing Fact from Opinion

Every day you are called upon to sort out fact and opinion. When a friend says she saw Mel Gibson's greatest movie last night, she is giving you her opinion. When she says she saw Mel Gibson's latest movie, she may be stating a fact. The fact can be proved—you can check to confirm or verify that the movie is indeed Mel Gibson's most recent film. The opinion can be disputed—ask around and others may not agree about the film's unqualified greatness. Because much of what you read and hear contains both facts and opinions, you need to be able to tell them apart. You need the skill of distinguishing fact from opinion.

Facts are statements that can be proved true. The proof must be objective and verifiable. You must be able to check for yourself to confirm a fact.

Look at the following facts. Notice that they can be checked for accuracy and confirmed. Suggested sources for verification appear in parentheses.

- In 1998 Bill Clinton was president of the United States. (Consult newspapers, news broadcasts, election results, etc.)

- Earth revolves around the sun. (Look it up in encyclopedias or astrological journals; ask knowledgeable people.)

- Dogs walk on four legs. (See for yourself.)

Opinions are statements that cannot be proved true. There is no objective evidence you can consult to check the truthfulness of an opinion. Unlike facts, opinions express personal beliefs or judgments. Opinions reveal how someone feels about a subject, not the facts about that subject. You might agree or disagree with someone's opinion, but you cannot prove it right or wrong.

Look at the following opinions. Reasons for classification as opinions appear in parentheses.

- Bill Clinton was born to be a president. (You cannot prove this by referring to birth records. There is no evidence to support this belief.)

- Intelligent life exists on other planets in our solar system. (There is no proof of this. It may be proved true some day, but for now it is just an educated guess—not a fact.)

- Dog is man's best friend. (This is not a fact; your best friend might not be a dog.)

As you read, be aware that facts and opinions are frequently mixed together. The following passage contains both facts and opinions:

> The new 2000 Cruising Yacht offers lots of real-life interior room. It
> features a luxuriant aft cabin, not some dim "cave." The galley comes

equipped with a full-size refrigerator and freezer. And this spacious galley has room to spare. The heads (there are two) have separate showers. The fit and finish are beyond equal and the performance is responsive and outstanding.

Did you detect that the third and fifth sentences state facts and that the rest of the sentences express opinions? Both facts and opinions are useful to you as a reader. But to evaluate what you read and to read intelligently, you need to know the difference between them.

## Keeping Events in Order

Writers organize details in a pattern. They present information in a certain order. Recognizing how writers organize—and understanding that organization—can help you improve your comprehension.

When details are arranged in the precise order in which they occurred, a writer is using a chronological (or time) pattern. A writer may, however, change this order. The story may "flash back" to past events that affected the present. The story may "flash forward" to show the results of present events. The writer may move back and forth between past, present, and future to help you see the importance of events.

## Making Correct Inferences

Much of what you read suggests more than it says. Writers do not always state outright what they want you to know. Frequently, they omit information that underlies the statements they make. They may assume that you already know it. They may want you to make the effort to figure out the implied information. To get the most out of what you read, you must come to an understanding about unstated information. You can do this through inference. From what is stated, you make inferences about what is not.

You make many inferences every day. Imagine, for example, that you are visiting a friend's house for the first time. You see a bag of dog food. You infer (make an inference) that the family has a dog. On another day you overhear a conversation. You catch the names of two actors and the words *scene, dialogue,* and *directing.* You infer that the people are discussing a movie or play.

In these situations and others like them, you infer unstated information from what you observe or read. Readers who cannot make inferences cannot see beyond the obvious. For the careful reader, facts are just the beginning. Facts stimulate your mind to think beyond them—to make an inference about what is meant but not stated.

The following passage is about Charles Dickens. As you read it, see how many inferences you can make.

Charles Dickens visited the United States in 1867. Wherever he went, the reception was the same. The night before, crowds arrived and lined up before the door. By morning the streets were campgrounds, with men, women, and children sitting or sleeping on blankets. Hustlers got ten times the price of a ticket. Once inside, audiences were surprised to hear their favorite Dickens characters speak with an English accent. After 76 readings Dickens boarded a ship for England. When his fellow passengers asked him to read, he said he'd rather be put in irons!

Did you notice that many inferences may be drawn from the passage? Dickens attracted huge crowds. From that fact you can infer that he was popular. His English accent surprised audiences. You can infer that many people didn't know he was English. Hustlers got high prices for tickets. This suggests that "scalping" tickets is not new. Dickens refused to read on the ship. You can infer that he was exhausted and tired of reading aloud to audiences. Those are some obvious inferences that can be made from the passage. More subtle ones can also be made; however, if you see the obvious ones, you understand how inferences are made.

Be careful about the inferences you make. One set of facts may suggest several inferences. Not all of them will be correct; some will be faulty inferences. The correct inference is supported by enough evidence to make it more likely than other inferences.

## Understanding Main Ideas

The main idea tells who or what is the subject of the paragraph or passage. The main idea is the most important idea, the idea that provides purpose and direction. The rest of the paragraph or passage explains, develops, or supports the main idea. Without a main idea, there would be only a collection of unconnected thoughts. It would be like a handle and a bowl without the "idea cup," or bread and meat without the "idea sandwich."

In the following passage, the main idea is printed in italics. As you read, observe how the other sentences develop or explain the main idea.

*Typhoon Chris hit with full fury today on the central coast of Japan.* Heavy rain from the storm flooded the area. High waves carried many homes into the sea. People now fear that the heavy rains will cause mudslides in the central part of the country. The number of people killed by the storm may climb past the 200 mark by Saturday.

In this paragraph, the main idea statement appears first. It is followed by sentences that explain, support, or give details. Sometimes the main idea appears at the end of a paragraph. Writers often construct that type of paragraph when their purpose is to persuade or convince. Readers may be more open to a new idea if the reasons for it are presented first. As you read the following paragraph, think about the overall impact of the supporting ideas. Their purpose is to convince the reader that the main idea in the last sentence should be accepted.

> Last week there was a head-on collision at Huntington and Canton streets. Just a month ago a pedestrian was struck there. Fortunately, she was only slightly injured. In the past year there have been more accidents there than at any other corner in the city. In fact, nearly 10 percent of all city accidents occur there. This intersection is dangerous, and a traffic signal should be installed there before a life is lost.

The details in the paragraph progress from least important to most important. They achieve their full effect in the main idea statement at the end.

In many cases, the main idea is not expressed in a single sentence. The reader is called upon to interpret all of the ideas expressed and decide upon a main idea. Read the following paragraph:

> The American author Jack London was once a pupil at the Cole Grammar School in Oakland, California. Each morning the class sang a song. When the teacher noticed that Jack wouldn't sing, she sent him to the principal. He returned to class with a note. It said that he could be excused from singing if he would write an essay every morning.

In this paragraph, the reader has to interpret the individual ideas and decide on a main idea. This main idea seems reasonable: Jack London's career as a writer began with a "punishment" in grammar school.

Understanding the concept of the main idea and knowing how to find it is important. Transferring that understanding to your reading and study is also important.

Many people take seasonal trips in search of a fair climate, good food, and a change of scene in pleasant surroundings. Some animals are impelled to travel for similar reasons. Their trips, too, are often annual and linked to the seasons. As the seasons change, they migrate to find food. These traveling animals are called migrants, and their trips are called migrations.

Most kinds of migrant animals make a round-trip each year. Grazing animals, particularly the hoofed animals of eastern Africa and the Arctic tundra, follow the seasonal changes in their search for green plants. Even fishes migrate. Some travel seasonally, and some travel less often. For example, eels and many salmon make a round-trip only once in their life cycle. These animals return to the home waters where they were born to lay eggs, and then they usually die.

Some animals make long journeys back and forth across land and ocean. Other migrations, however, take a vertical direction. During seasons of severe weather in mountainous regions, for instance, certain birds, insects, and mammals make regular trips from their breeding grounds in high altitudes into the foothills or plains below.

Many birds become gregarious during their travels. Even those that are fiercely individualistic at other times, such as birds of prey and those that hunt insects, often travel with birds that have similar habits. Large migrating flocks may be seen scattered along a broad flyway hundreds of miles wide. Often the birds show remarkable grouping. The most characteristic migratory formation is the V-shape of a flock of geese, ducks, pelicans, or cranes, the V pointed in the direction of the flight. Birds usually follow specific, well-defined routes over long distances marked by rivers, valleys, coasts, forests, plains, deserts, and other geographic features. However, birds may change routes because of wind and weather. The routes of some of the larger birds span oceans. Even small birds may cross as many as 1,000 miles (1,600 kilometers) of water over the Gulf of Mexico, the Mediterranean Sea, or the North Sea.

In the fall, female shorebirds often depart first, leaving the males to care for the young. In other species, male birds migrate first. They fly ahead to select the nesting site in preparation for the arrival of the females. Sometimes males and females travel together and may choose mates along the way. Geese, who mate for life, travel as couples in large flocks.

**Reading Time** _____

## Recalling Facts

1. Most migrant animals
   - ❏ a. make a round-trip each year.
   - ❏ b. make a round-trip once in their life cycle.
   - ❏ c. die after they migrate.

2. Most animals migrate because of
   - ❏ a. boredom.
   - ❏ b. food availability and seasonal changes.
   - ❏ c. a need to return home.

3. Migrating birds usually travel
   - ❏ a. wherever the wind takes them.
   - ❏ b. alone.
   - ❏ c. over specific, well-defined routes.

4. The most characteristic migratory formation for birds is the
   - ❏ a. A-formation.
   - ❏ b. V-formation.
   - ❏ c. W-formation.

5. In some species, male birds migrate before the females so that they can
   - ❏ a. select the nesting site.
   - ❏ b. fend off enemies.
   - ❏ c. stockpile food.

## Understanding Ideas

6. If climate and food supply remained constant, most animals would probably
   - ❏ a. stay in one place.
   - ❏ b. continue to migrate.
   - ❏ c. change their eating habits.

7. From the selection, you can conclude that many birds of prey usually
   - ❏ a. hunt alone.
   - ❏ b. live in large flocks.
   - ❏ c. migrate alone.

8. Even small birds can fly over vast amounts of water during migration, which suggests that
   - ❏ a. there is a strong correlation between size and endurance.
   - ❏ b. smaller birds have more endurance than larger birds.
   - ❏ c. size and endurance are not related.

9. Whether male and female birds migrate together depends on
   - ❏ a. breeding habits.
   - ❏ b. flying ability.
   - ❏ c. location north.

10. Birds migrate over specific routes, which suggests that
    - ❏ a. all migrating animals follow the same routes.
    - ❏ b. birds are able to remember previous migrations.
    - ❏ c. migrations are dependent on geographic features.

# Migrant Insect

In 1975, an American couple named Ken and Catalina Brugger were climbing in the mountains of central Mexico when they came upon an awesome sight: hundreds of thousands of monarch butterflies clinging to the branches of fir trees. The Bruggers had found the winter home of the eastern race of monarch butterflies, perhaps the world's most famous migrating insect.

Each year in early spring, the monarchs set out from their winter home, traveling north and laying their eggs on milkweed. After they lay their eggs, they die. As the eggs hatch, the caterpillars feed on the milkweed, the only thing they ingest. Eventually, the caterpillars become butterflies, and they, too, travel northward, laying their own eggs as they go. By early summer, the monarchs, perhaps three generations removed from those that wintered in Mexico, reach Canada.

In late summer, millions of monarch butterflies head south, catching air currents to speed them on their way. Their flight may seem random to humans, but one tagged monarch traveled over 230 miles (370.3 kilometers) in one day. Eventually, they reach their winter home, where the climate enables them to live in a state of near hibernation until it is time to head north again the following spring.

1. **Recognizing Words in Context**

    Find the word *ingest* in the passage. One definition below is a *synonym* for that word; it means the same or almost the same thing. One definition is an *antonym;* it has the opposite or nearly opposite meaning. The other has a completely different meaning. Label the definitions S for *synonym,* A for *antonym,* and D for *different.*

    _____ a. eat

    _____ b. destroy

    _____ c. reject

2. **Distinguishing Fact from Opinion**

    Two of the statements below present *facts,* which can be proved correct. The other statement is an *opinion,* which expresses someone's thoughts or beliefs. Label the statements F for *fact* and O for *opinion.*

    _____ a. Eastern monarchs winter in Mexico.

    _____ b. Monarchs are the world's most famous migrating insect.

    _____ c. One butterfly traveled over two hundred miles (322 kilometers) in a day.

## 3. Keeping Events in Order

Label the statements below 1, 2, and 3 to show the order in which the events happened.

_____ a. Monarchs fly south to Mexico.

_____ b. Monarchs lay their eggs on milkweed.

_____ c. Monarchs head north as the milkweed sprouts.

## 4. Making Correct Inferences

Two of the statements below are correct *inferences*, or reasonable guesses. They are based on information in the passage. The other statement is an incorrect, or faulty, inference. Label the statements C for *correct* inference and F for *faulty* inference.

_____ a. The migration of the monarch is an amazing feat.

_____ b. The same monarchs make the trip year after year.

_____ c. Monarchs live less than one full year.

## 5. Understanding Main Ideas

One of the statements below expresses the main idea of the passage. One statement is too general, or too broad. The other explains only part of the passage; it is too narrow. Label the statements M for *main idea*, B for *too broad*, and N for *too narrow*.

_____ a. The winter home of the monarch butterfly was finally found in 1975.

_____ b. Eastern monarch butterflies migrate every year.

_____ c. Monarch migration from Mexico to Canada and back follows a predictable pattern.

Correct Answers, Part A _____

Correct Answers, Part B _____

Total Correct Answers _____

When fossil fuels such as coal, gasoline, and fuel oils are burned, they emit oxides of sulfur, carbon, and nitrogen into the air. These oxides combine with moisture in the air to form sulfuric acid, carbonic acid, and nitric acid. When it rains or snows, these acids fall on the earth in what is called acid rain.

During the 20th century, the acidity of the air and acid rain have come to be recognized as leading threats to the stability and quality of Earth's environment. Most of this acidity is produced in the industrialized nations of the Northern Hemisphere—the United States, Canada, Japan, and many countries of Europe.

The effects of acid rain can be devastating to many forms of life, including human life. Its effects can be most vividly seen, however, in lakes, rivers, and streams. Acidity in water kills virtually all life forms. By the early 1990s, tens of thousands of lakes had been destroyed by acid rain. The problem has been most severe in Norway, Sweden, and Canada.

Scientists use what is called the pH factor to measure the acidity or alkalinity of liquid solutions. On a scale from 0 to 14, the number 0 represents the highest level of acid. 14 represents the most basic or alkaline. Rainfalls in the eastern United States and in Western Europe often have a pH factor ranging from 4.5 to 4.0.

The threat posed by acid rain is not limited by geographic boundaries. Prevailing winds carry the pollutants around the globe. For example, much research supports the conclusion that pollution from coal-powered electric generating stations in the midwestern United States is the ultimate cause of the severe acid-rain problem in eastern Canada and the northeastern United States. Nor are the destructive effects of acid rain limited to the natural environment. Structures made of stone, metal, and cement have also been damaged or destroyed. Some of the world's great monuments have shown signs of deterioration. This deterioration is probably caused by acid rain.

The cost of antipollution equipment such as burners, filters, and chemical and washing devices is great. However, the cost in damage to the environment and human life is estimated to be much greater because the damage caused by acid rain may be irreversible. Although preventive measures are being taken, up to 500,000 lakes in North America may be destroyed before the end of the 20th century.

**Reading Time** _____

17

## Recalling Facts

1. Acid rain originates from
   - ❏ a. freezing water.
   - ❏ b. burning fossil fuels.
   - ❏ c. the natural environment.

2. The acidity of liquid solutions is measured by
   - ❏ a. rainfall amounts.
   - ❏ b. electrical generators.
   - ❏ c. the pH factor.

3. Acid rain is a threat to lakes because
   - ❏ a. acidity in water kills virtually all life forms.
   - ❏ b. it causes water to overflow its banks.
   - ❏ c. the water becomes too alkaline.

4. The effects of acid rain are not limited by geographic boundaries because
   - ❏ a. it rains everywhere.
   - ❏ b. prevailing winds carry pollutants around the globe.
   - ❏ c. antipollution equipment is too costly.

5. It is estimated that by the end of the 20th century,
   - ❏ a. up to 100,000 lakes in North America may be destroyed.
   - ❏ b. up to 300,000 lakes in North America may be destroyed.
   - ❏ c. up to 500,000 lakes in North America may be destroyed.

## Understanding Ideas

6. You can conclude from the article that acid rain
   - ❏ a. is a problem that cannot be solved by one country alone.
   - ❏ b. is a threat that cannot be eliminated.
   - ❏ c. is the most important problem facing the world.

7. You can conclude that the destruction of lakes by acid rain has been most severe where
   - ❏ a. there is the most industry.
   - ❏ b. the level of acidity in rainfall is the highest.
   - ❏ c. wind is the strongest.

8. You can conclude from the article that lakes are destroyed by acid rain because
   - ❏ a. lakes cannot exist without life forms in the water.
   - ❏ b. acidity kills the water.
   - ❏ c. surrounding vegetation is killed.

9. You can conclude from the article that the only way to reverse the effects of acid rain is through
   - ❏ a. education.
   - ❏ b. antipollution equipment.
   - ❏ c. measuring water acidity.

10. The most devastating effects of acid rain may eventually be
    - ❏ a. loss of all rivers, lakes, and streams.
    - ❏ b. destruction of great monuments.
    - ❏ c. loss of human life.

# Deadly Rain

For eleven and a half months of the year, the blue-spotted salamander lives underground, feeding on bugs, worms, and other underground creatures. Once a year—on a dark, wet night in late March or early April—the blue-spot emerges from its underground home. It makes its way to its temporary home, a pond, where it mates and lays its eggs.

Once, biology students keeping track of the salamander population could count more than fifty blue-spots a night at one of these breeding ponds. Gradually, the students began to notice a decline in the blue-spot population. Within ten years, no salamanders visited the pond at all. As it turned out, biologists specializing in amphibians had noticed similar drops in the salamander population all over the Northeast United States.

What caused these drops? Acid rain caused by smokestack emissions in the industrial triangle of Chicago, Detroit, and Pittsburgh was creating a chemical imbalance in the waters of the ponds where the salamanders bred. Blue-spotted salamanders are now almost extinct in many northeastern states.

The disappearance of the blue-spotted salamander sends a clear message. Salamanders are considered an indicator species. When they begin to disappear, it is a sign that some broader ecological upset is at work that can affect humans as well as other animals and plants. We need to heed the warning.

## 1. Recognizing Words in Context

Find the word *drops* in the passage. One definition below is a *synonym* for that word; it means the same or almost the same thing. One definition is an *antonym;* it has the opposite or nearly opposite meaning. The other has a completely different meaning. Label the definitions S for *synonym,* A for *antonym,* and D for *different.*

_____ a. increases

_____ b. decreases

_____ c. departures

## 2. Distinguishing Fact from Opinion

Two of the statements below present *facts,* which can be proved correct. The other statement is an *opinion,* which expresses someone's thoughts or beliefs. Label the statements F for *fact* and O for *opinion.*

_____ a. The blue-spotted salamander decreased in numbers in the Northeast.

_____ b. We need to heed the warning.

_____ c. Biology students counted more than fifty salamanders a night.

## 3. Keeping Events in Order

Two of the statements below describe events that happened at the same time. The other statement describes an event that happened before or after those events. Label them S for *same time*, B for *before*, and A for *after*.

_____ a. Acid rain created a chemical imbalance in the water of the ponds where salamanders bred.

_____ b. The numbers of salamanders declined.

_____ c. Biology students counted more than fifty salamanders a night at one pond.

## 4. Making Correct Inferences

Two of the statements below are correct *inferences*, or reasonable guesses. They are based on information in the passage. The other statement is an incorrect, or faulty, inference. Label the statements C for *correct* inference and F for *faulty* inference.

_____ a. Humans heeded the warning sent by the salamanders.

_____ b. Acid rain caused the disappearance of the salamanders.

_____ c. What happened to the salamanders could have an effect on people.

## 5. Understanding Main Ideas

One of the statements below expresses the main idea of the passage. One statement is too general, or too broad. The other explains only part of the passage; it is too narrow. Label the statements M for *main idea*, B for *too broad*, and N for *too narrow*.

_____ a. Acid rain has caused worldwide problems.

_____ b. Acid rain has caused a decline in the population of blue-spotted salamanders.

_____ c. Within ten years, no salamanders visited the pond.

Correct Answers, Part A _____

Correct Answers, Part B _____

Total Correct Answers _____

# 3 A  A Romantic Weapon?

The "most romantic of weapons," the sword has been the symbol of war and the badge of honor and courage among fighting men since the days when bronze and iron were first hammered into blades. The right to carry a sword has almost always been a mark of rank. Even today, when most of its usefulness has passed, the sword remains part of the dress uniform of army and navy officers throughout the world.

In the days of chivalry, knighthood was conferred by laying the flat of the sword on the young warrior's shoulder. In many lands, kissing the ruler's sword was a token of homage. Oaths taken by a soldier on his sword were rigidly binding. When a general surrendered his sword, he admitted complete defeat. And to have one's sword broken by a superior officer was one of the worst degradations that could come to the disloyal or cowardly soldier. These and many other sword ceremonies reappear constantly in history. The mythologies and folklore of many nations contain tales of magic swords, like King Arthur's Excalibur.

In modern warfare, the work of the sword is mostly done by the bayonet fastened to the rifle muzzle or used as a dagger. For many centuries, however, and even for some time after the invention of firearms, the sword in one or another of its many forms was the principal weapon of fighters. Instead of doing away with the sword, the invention of firearms resulted in a diversity of the types of swords used in combat.

The heavy two-handed sword of the Middle Ages was abandoned as soon as the invention of firearms destroyed the usefulness of armor. The place of the two-handed sword was taken by the saber, the rapier, and the smallsword. With these lighter blades, swordsmanship became a fine art. During the 17th and 18th centuries in Europe, it became the custom for all men, even civilians, to carry swords, and quarrels were usually settled on the spot. During the reign of Louis XIII in France, dueling became such a rage that fencing masters were in great demand and highly honored. Earlier, duels were fought with sword in one hand and dagger, for parrying, in the other. Later, a cloak took the place of the dagger.

Sword making used to be one of the most honorable trades. In many nations today, it remains a highly honored craft.

**Reading Time** _____

## Recalling Facts

1. The right to carry a sword has almost always been a
   - ❏ a. duty.
   - ❏ b. token of homage.
   - ❏ c. mark of rank.

2. Knighthood was conferred by
   - ❏ a. laying the sword on a warrior's shoulder.
   - ❏ b. kissing a sword.
   - ❏ c. breaking a sword in half.

3. In folklore, Excalibur is the name of King Arthur's
   - ❏ a. army.
   - ❏ b. magic sword.
   - ❏ c. chief knight.

4. In modern warfare, the work of a sword is mostly done by
   - ❏ a. firearms.
   - ❏ b. sabers.
   - ❏ c. bayonets.

5. Armor became useless when
   - ❏ a. swords were no longer made.
   - ❏ b. firearms were invented.
   - ❏ c. fencing became a popular pastime.

## Understanding Ideas

6. It was degrading to have one's sword broken by a superior because the sword
   - ❏ a. was expensive to replace.
   - ❏ b. was a useful weapon.
   - ❏ c. was a symbol of honor.

7. After firearms were invented, swords continued to be used in battle. This suggests that
   - ❏ a. soldiers did not like firearms.
   - ❏ b. firearms were too expensive.
   - ❏ c. swords were effective weapons.

8. Carrying swords became popular among civilians when
   - ❏ a. dueling became the rage in Europe.
   - ❏ b. swords became lighter and more diversified.
   - ❏ c. soldiers started using firearms.

9. What does the article suggest about the art of sword making today?
   - ❏ a. The trade is not as highly honored as it once was.
   - ❏ b. Making swords does not pay well.
   - ❏ c. Some nations have outlawed sword making.

10. The article implies that today swords are viewed primarily as
    - ❏ a. symbols of honor and courage.
    - ❏ b. useful weapons in battle.
    - ❏ c. symbols of death and destruction.

Carrying a heavy duffel bag, Steve Mason mounts the stairs to a "fight studio." Steve is an aspiring actor, and part of his theatrical training includes the art of stage fighting.

Steve and his fight partner don protective padding and pick up their swords. Today, they are practicing a battle scene for a play by William Shakespeare. First, they study the intricate fight plan. Every step in a stage fight is precisely choreographed; there can be no surprises. The partners move backward, forward, and around each other according to the elaborate plan. The actors must make the fight look and sound real—grunts and cries are part of the plan, as are exaggerated reactions and pretend hits. They swing their heavy swords, which are dull and have guards at the tip, and block each other's thrusts. Actors suffer few cuts in stage fighting, but many bruises.

This fight plan calls for Steve to die during the battle. As his partner vigorously thrusts his sword at him, Steve catches the weapon between his body and his arm and falls backward. From the perspective of the audience, it should look as if the sword has gone through his body, mortally wounding him.

After the strenuous rehearsal, Steve and his partner stow their swords and remove their protective padding. They will return tomorrow to reenact the deadly battle—realistic stage fighting takes a lot of practice and discipline.

## 1. Recognizing Words in Context

Find the word *don* in the passage. One definition below is a *synonym* for that word; it means the same or almost the same thing. One definition is an *antonym;* it has the opposite or nearly opposite meaning. The other has a completely different meaning. Label the definitions S for *synonym,* A for *antonym,* and D for *different.*

_____ a. take off

_____ b. put on

_____ c. expect

## 2. Distinguishing Fact from Opinion

Two of the statements below present facts, which can be proved correct. The other statement is an opinion, which expresses someone's thoughts or beliefs. Label the statements F for *fact* and O for *opinion.*

_____ a. The swords have guards at the tip.

_____ b. The fight is planned in advance.

_____ c. The fight will look real to the audience.

### 3. Keeping Events in Order

Label the statements below 1, 2, and 3 to show the order in which the events happened.

_____ a. Steve practices dying on stage.

_____ b. Steve puts on protective padding.

_____ c. Steve and his partner practice their moves.

### 4. Making Correct Inferences

Two of the statements below are correct *inferences*, or reasonable guesses. They are based on information in the passage. The other statement is an incorrect, or faulty, inference. Label the statements C for *correct* inference and F for *faulty* inference.

_____ a. Stage fighting is hard physical work.

_____ b. It is impossible to get hurt in a stage fight.

_____ c. A stage fight requires more acting than actual fighting.

### 5. Understanding Main Ideas

One of the statements below expresses the main idea of the passage. One statement is too general, or too broad. The other explains only part of the passage; it is too narrow. Label the statements M for *main idea,* B for *too broad,* and N for *too narrow.*

_____ a. Stage fights are interesting.

_____ b. Much work and preparation go into a stage fight.

_____ c. Steve practices his fighting technique regularly.

Correct Answers, Part A _____

Correct Answers, Part B _____

Total Correct Answers _____

The relatively large natural bodies that revolve around, or orbit, the sun are called planets. The term *planet* does not include such smaller bodies as comets, meteors, and asteroids, many of which are little more than pieces of ice or rock. The sun, the nine planets, their satellites, and all the smaller bodies, particles, and dust that circle the sun form the solar system. The sun, near the center of the solar system, governs the planets' orbital motions by gravitational attraction. It also provides the planets with light and heat.

In order of increasing distance from the sun, the nine planets of the solar system are Mercury, Venus, Earth, Mars, Jupiter, Saturn, Uranus, Neptune, and Pluto. Mercury, Venus, Mars, Jupiter, and Saturn can be seen without a telescope. Although Uranus is also sometimes visible without a telescope, ancient astronomers were unable to distinguish it from true stars.

The planets may be divided in several ways. Mercury and Venus, which revolve around the sun in orbits smaller in diameter than that of the Earth, are classified as inferior planets. The so-called superior planets are those that revolve around the sun in orbits larger in diameter than the Earth's orbit. The planets may also be classified according to their gross physical characteristics. The terrestrial, or Earthlike, planets are close to the sun and are composed primarily of rock and metal. They include Mercury, Venus, Earth, and Mars. The terrestrial planets are also called the inner planets.

The Jovian, or Jupiterlike, planets are very large compared to the terrestrial planets and are much farther from the sun. They include Jupiter, Saturn, Uranus, and Neptune. These planets are composed mostly of hydrogen and helium in gaseous and liquid forms. Pluto, the outermost planet, is usually considered neither a terrestrial nor a Jovian planet. Composed of ice and rock, Pluto is much smaller than the other planets.

Although the origin of the solar system is uncertain, most scientists believe that it began to develop about four and a half billion years ago from a large cloud of gas and dust. The cloud began to contract. As the material within the cloud became compressed, it grew hot. Most of this mass was drawn toward the center of the cloud, eventually forming the sun. The remaining material formed a spinning disk around the center. The planets and satellites evolved from this material as it cooled.

**Reading Time** _____

**Recalling Facts**

1. Planets are held in their orbits by
   - ❏ a. gravitational attraction to each other.
   - ❏ b. the sun's gravitational attraction.
   - ❏ c. the gravitational attraction of the moon.

2. The sun provides the planets with
   - ❏ a. water and light.
   - ❏ b. air and light.
   - ❏ c. light and heat.

3. The planet farthest from the sun is
   - ❏ a. Mercury.
   - ❏ b. Pluto.
   - ❏ c. Saturn.

4. The Jovian planets are also called
   - ❏ a. inner planets.
   - ❏ b. terrestrial planets.
   - ❏ c. superior planets.

5. The planets most like the Earth are called
   - ❏ a. orbital planets.
   - ❏ b. outer planets.
   - ❏ c. terrestrial planets.

**Understanding Ideas**

6. You can conclude from the article that all terrestrial planets are
   - ❏ a. inner planets.
   - ❏ b. superior planets.
   - ❏ c. inferior planets.

7. The article suggests that ancient astronomers
   - ❏ a. were familiar with all nine planets.
   - ❏ b. knew about only six planets.
   - ❏ c. thought all the planets were stars.

8. You can conclude from the article that without a telescope, you could not see
   - ❏ a. Uranus, Neptune, and Pluto.
   - ❏ b. Neptune and Pluto.
   - ❏ c. most of the planets.

9. Humans' knowledge of the origin of the solar system
   - ❏ a. is scientific fact.
   - ❏ b. is speculation based on scientific principles.
   - ❏ c. is based on stories from ancient astronomers.

10. You can conclude from the article that the invention of the telescope
   - ❏ a. greatly increased our knowledge of the solar system.
   - ❏ b. explained the origin of the solar system.
   - ❏ c. made astronomy a science.

Clyde Tombaugh, a 22-year-old former farmer with no advanced degrees, discovered the solar system's ninth planet, Pluto. As a boy, Tombaugh was interested in astronomy and had built his own telescope. He drew pictures of what he saw through it of the planet Jupiter and sent them to Lowell Observatory on an impulse. Impressed with Tombaugh's observations, the observatory's director invited Tombaugh to try out as an assistant. "I couldn't fail," Tombaugh later recalled. "I had only enough money for one-way train fare."

In 1929, Lowell Observatory had begun a systematic search for what astronomers called Planet X. Thousands of photographs were taken of small segments of the sky several days apart. Matched pairs of pictures were placed in a stereoscopic device called a blink comparator. Fixed stars remained in the same position with each blink; anything that moved—such as a planet—would be revealed against the steady background of stars. Tombaugh toiled over the plates for months without success. Then on February 18, 1930, he saw an image that moved. "The object was far beyond the orbit of Neptune," Tombaugh wrote. "A terrific thrill came over me."

After rechecking his findings, Tombaugh went to the director's office and reported, "Dr. Slipher, I have found your Planet X."

### 1. Recognizing Words in Context

Find the word *toiled* in the passage. One definition below is a *synonym* for that word; it means the same or almost the same thing. One definition is an *antonym*; it has the opposite or nearly opposite meaning. The other has a completely different meaning. Label the definitions S for *synonym*, A for *antonym*, and D for *different*.

_____ a. rested

_____ b. battled

_____ c. labored

### 2. Distinguishing Fact from Opinion

Two of the statements below present *facts*, which can be proved correct. The other statement is an *opinion*, which expresses someone's thoughts or beliefs. Label the statements F for *fact* and O for *opinion*.

_____ a. Tombaugh had no formal training as an astronomer.

_____ b. Tombaugh discovered the ninth planet, Pluto.

_____ c. Tombaugh was daring to send his sketches to Lowell Observatory.

## 3. Keeping Events in Order

Label the statements below 1, 2, and 3 to show the order in which the events happened.

_____ a. Tombaugh saw a moving image.

_____ b. Photographs were taken of sections of the sky.

_____ c. Tombaugh compared photographs using the blink comparator.

## 4. Making Correct Inferences

Two of the statements below are correct *inferences*, or reasonable guesses. They are based on information in the passage. The other statement is an incorrect, or faulty, inference. Label the statements C for *correct* inference and F for *faulty* inference.

_____ a. It does not take scientific training to become a good astronomer.

_____ b. Clyde Tombaugh made his discovery through hard work and persistence.

_____ c. The observatory director thought that Tombaugh had the potential to become an astronomer.

## 5. Understanding Main Ideas

One of the statements below expresses the main idea of the passage. One statement is too general, or too broad. The other explains only part of the passage; it is too narrow. Label the statements M for *main idea*, B for *too broad*, and N for *too narrow*.

_____ a. Clyde Tombaugh discovered the solar system's ninth planet.

_____ b. Moving objects in space are discovered by using a machine called a blink comparator.

_____ c. For generations, astronomers have been searching for new planets.

Correct Answers, Part A _____

Correct Answers, Part B _____

Total Correct Answers _____

The Changing Zoo

A park where captive animals, often from all over the world, live is a zoo. The word *zoo* comes from the word *zoology*—"the science of animals." At the zoo, visitors can see exhibits of often strange and always fascinating animals from lands both near and far. Few people find it possible to visit such exotic places as the jungles of Asia or the grasslands of Africa to see the animals whose homes are there. Many people who live in cities cannot visit farms or the wilderness areas of their own country. The zoo provides opportunities for people to see wild animals.

Zoos today are also becoming sanctuaries for vanishing wildlife. Rapidly growing human populations are destroying many retreats of wild animals. Unless they are protected, many animals may become extinct within the next few generations. Modern zoos are providing just such protection. By breeding threatened species in captivity, they may save rare animals from extinction.

Many older zoos are parks with fenced enclosures and buildings containing caged animals. Lions, tigers, and other cats are kept in one house; monkeys in another. However, animals in bare cages with little room to move are not very interesting to watch. Modern zoos are different; they dramatize the animals by displaying them in surroundings that resemble their natural environments.

Visitors to a modern zoo can look across a small open plain and see lions apparently free to wander about as they please. Nearby are ostriches, cranes, antelopes, and zebras feeding quietly at the edge of a water hole. These animals of prey are not afraid of the lions because they are separated from them by wide, deep trenches, or moats. Moats also separate the visitors from the animals in the exhibit. Visitors often cannot see the moats because they are hidden by plants. Because the moats are not easily seen, visitors can feel that they are seeing the animals living wild in their natural settings.

Experience has shown that lions cannot jump as far as 30 feet (9 meters) in a straight line and 6 feet (1.8 meters) upward. They can be held on a sort of island by moats about 35 feet (10.5 meters) wide with a wall at least 6 feet (1.8 meters) high. However, pumas and leopards make tremendous leaps; consequently, they must be kept in cages.

Zoologists feel that today's zoos are more "animal friendly" than those of the past.

**Reading Time** _____

## Recalling Facts

1. The word *zoology* means
   - ❏ a. a park of captive animals.
   - ❏ b. the natural habitat of animals.
   - ❏ c. the science of animals.

2. Animals that must be caged in zoos include
   - ❏ a. ostriches and lions.
   - ❏ b. pumas and leopards.
   - ❏ c. antelopes and zebras.

3. A moat is a
   - ❏ a. wide, deep trench.
   - ❏ b. type of cage.
   - ❏ c. shallow hole.

4. Growing human populations are
   - ❏ a. helping to save wild animals.
   - ❏ b. destroying many animal retreats.
   - ❏ c. living happily with wild animals.

5. As leapers, lions can
   - ❏ a. leap higher than any other animal.
   - ❏ b. not leap as high as leopards.
   - ❏ c. make longer jumps than leopards.

## Understanding Ideas

6. The article wants you to understand that animals in zoos
   - ❏ a. should be returned to the wild.
   - ❏ b. are a resource for people who cannot travel to see animals.
   - ❏ c. are becoming extinct.

7. The article suggests that the extinction of wild animals
   - ❏ a. cannot be stopped.
   - ❏ b. is part of nature's plan.
   - ❏ c. may be stopped if the animals are protected.

8. You can conclude that in order to save animals from extinction humans should
   - ❏ a. stop visiting zoos.
   - ❏ b. limit their population.
   - ❏ c. support the protection and breeding of endangered animals.

9. Zoos use moats to
   - ❏ a. provide water for animals.
   - ❏ b. save money on cages.
   - ❏ c. reduce the threat of animals to each other.

10. Why are modern zoos more "animal friendly" than those of the past?
    - ❏ a. Human populations are destroying many animal retreats.
    - ❏ b. When possible, animals are in their natural settings.
    - ❏ c. Older zoos were not very interesting.

# Saving the Condor

In a zoo laboratory in Los Angeles, California, a large, ugly California condor chick sits waiting for its breakfast. That breakfast—aged raw meat—arrives from behind a screen in the beak of a hand puppet shaped like an adult condor. Behind the screen, manipulating the puppet, is the chick's keeper. The chick grabs the meat and gobbles it down.

When a female condor at the Los Angeles Zoo lays an egg, zookeepers take it to hatch artificially; with luck, the female will lay another, and even a third. This technique has allowed the zoo to double and even triple its number of condor chicks. Some of the condors will remain in the zoo, but others will be released in an effort to reestablish the wild condor population.

Within six months, the fuzzy chick is a twenty-pound (nine-kilogram) juvenile ready to fly. Then it graduates to a flight pen large enough to accommodate its nine-foot (2.7-meter) wingspan.

If conditions are right, one day this young condor will soar over the mountains of California or Arizona. Otherwise it will remain under the protection of the zoo, a leader in the captive condor breeding program in cooperation with the United States Fish and Wildlife Service.

## 1. Recognizing Words in Context

Find the word *reestablish* in the passage. One definition below is a *synonym* for that word; it means the same or almost the same thing. One definition is an *antonym;* it has the opposite or nearly opposite meaning. The other has a completely different meaning. Label the definitions S for *synonym,* A for *antonym,* and D for *different.*

_____ a. put back

_____ b. remove

_____ c. echo

## 2. Distinguishing Fact from Opinion

Two of the statements below present *facts,* which can be proved correct. The other statement is an *opinion,* which expresses someone's thoughts or beliefs. Label the statements F for *fact* and O for *opinion.*

_____ a. Condor chicks are ugly.

_____ b. Condors have a nine-foot (2.7-meter) wingspan.

_____ c. Zookeepers take condor eggs to hatch artificially.

### 3. Keeping Events in Order

Label the statements below 1, 2, and 3 to show the order in which the events happened.

_____ a. Condor chicks are fed by using a hand puppet.

_____ b. Zookeepers take condor eggs away from female condors.

_____ c. The young condors are released into the wild.

### 4. Making Correct Inferences

Two of the statements below are correct *inferences,* or reasonable guesses. They are based on information in the passage. The other statement is an incorrect, or faulty, inference. Label the statements C for *correct* inference and F for *faulty* inference.

_____ a. The Los Angeles Zoo is active in saving the condor.

_____ b. All hand-raised condors can be released into the wild.

_____ c. Raising condors for release requires skill and knowledge.

### 5. Understanding Main Ideas

One of the statements below expresses the main idea of the passage. One statement is too general, or too broad. The other explains only part of the passage; it is too narrow. Label the statements M for *main idea,* B for *too broad,* and N for *too narrow.*

_____ a. Zoos help to save endangered species.

_____ b. The Los Angeles Zoo is helping to restore condors to the wild.

_____ c. Condor eggs can be taken from parents and hatched artificially.

Correct Answers, Part A _____

Correct Answers, Part B _____

Total Correct Answers _____

Located in northeastern Africa in an area known as the Horn of Africa, Ethiopia is one of the continent's largest and most populous countries. Ethiopia's landscape varies from lowlands to high plateaus. Its climate ranges from very dry to seasonally very wet. The Ethiopian population is also very mixed. There are broad differences in cultural background and traits. Methods of gaining a livelihood, languages, and religions all differ from place to place.

While occasionally occupied by other nations, Ethiopia is one of the few countries in Africa never truly colonized. Since World War II, Ethiopia has often been economically, politically, or militarily dependent on the major world powers. Its substantial trade deficit has been attributed to internal disorder.

The landscape of Ethiopia is dominated by central highlands of plateaus and mountains. Surrounding the highlands are hot and usually arid lowlands. The highlands are cut by deep river valleys. Situated in the tropics, Ethiopia has climatic regions that vary with elevation. Daily temperatures range seasonally from well above 100° F (40° C) in the lowlands to below freezing in the cooler upland elevations and higher.

Moisture is also unevenly distributed. Most areas have regular wet and dry periods during the year. The amount of rainfall often depends on altitude. The higher areas are wetter; the lowlands drier. At times, rains may start later or end earlier than usual. Storms may be separated by a few weeks, allowing the soil to dry out. Such drought is most common in the northern and eastern highlands and in lowland areas. When this happens, farming and herding suffer, which can lead to famine.

Ethiopia's most valuable natural resource is the soil. Although it is potentially highly productive for traditional and modern agriculture, this potential is largely unmet. In parts of Ethiopia, the soil suffers from declining fertility and erosion. The decline results from the continuous inefficient use of the soil. Farmers cultivate land that is better for grazing or land that should be left unplanted for a time. But the socioeconomic system does not reward investment in soil protection. There are also the increasing demands of a rapidly growing population. As a consequence, agricultural production per person has declined in the late 20th century.

Little has been done to find possible mineral resources in Ethiopia. Those known include gold, platinum, manganese, and salt. There is little extraction of either metallic ores or mineral fuels.

**Reading Time** _____

## Recalling Facts

1. Ethiopia is located in
   - ❏ a. western Africa.
   - ❏ b. southern Africa.
   - ❏ c. northeastern Africa.

2. Ethiopia's most valuable natural resource is
   - ❏ a. mineral fuels.
   - ❏ b. soil.
   - ❏ c. metallic ores.

3. One cause of the decline in agricultural production per person is
   - ❏ a. famine.
   - ❏ b. decreased population.
   - ❏ c. inefficient use of soil.

4. Mineral resources in Ethiopia include gold and
   - ❏ a. salt.
   - ❏ b. soil.
   - ❏ c. silver.

5. Ethiopian people are
   - ❏ a. culturally varied.
   - ❏ b. similar in background.
   - ❏ c. very religious.

## Understanding Ideas

6. From the article, you can conclude that Ethiopia is a country of
   - ❏ a. moderation.
   - ❏ b. extremes.
   - ❏ c. constancy.

7. Ethiopia could be described as
   - ❏ a. economically backward.
   - ❏ b. technologically advanced.
   - ❏ c. industrialized.

8. The article suggests that a solution to Ethiopia's problems is
   - ❏ a. increased population.
   - ❏ b. planned soil protection.
   - ❏ c. increased logging.

9. Politically, Ethiopia can be characterized as
   - ❏ a. democratic.
   - ❏ b. stable.
   - ❏ c. unstable.

10. You can conclude from the article that
    - ❏ a. there are many mineral resources in Ethiopia.
    - ❏ b. Ethiopia is a self-sufficient country.
    - ❏ c. Ethiopia cannot provide enough food to feed its growing population.

## 6 | B | The Lost Ark

According to tradition, the lost Ark of the Covenant was a chest holding the tablet of the Ten Commandments. It is said that the Ark was carried out of Egypt by the Hebrews during their desert wanderings with Moses. They placed the Ark in the Temple of Solomon in Jerusalem, but it vanished mysteriously. The Ark was never seen again.

Ethiopians, however, say that Menelik, the son of King Solomon and the queen of Sheba, brought the Ark to Ethiopia with him. They say that they have kept it in a secret place ever since.

This Ethiopian legend may contain a germ of truth. When Egypt ruled Jerusalem, a colony of Jews in the south remained faithful. They may have sheltered the Ark. But when their colony was destroyed, the people disappeared.

Scholars hypothesize that these people moved south to Ethiopia. Further support for this theory is given by the fact that Ethiopia has a small population of Jews who cling to an ancient form of Judaism. These people, the Falashas, claim to be a lost tribe of Israel, led out of Egypt by Abba Musie, or Moses.

First the rule of Ethiopian emperors, then revolution and political unrest prevented investigators from following up the pieces of the puzzle. But it continues to tantalize researchers. Might the lost Ark one day be found in Ethiopia?

1. **Recognizing Words in Context**

   Find the word *hypothesize* in the passage. One definition below is a *synonym* for that word; it means the same or almost the same thing. One definition is an *antonym*; it has the opposite or nearly opposite meaning. The other has a completely different meaning. Label the definitions S for *synonym*, A for *antonym*, and D for *different*.

   _____ a. doubt

   _____ b. theorize

   _____ c. discover

2. **Distinguishing Fact from Opinion**

   Two of the statements below present *facts*, which can be proved correct. The other statement is an *opinion*, which expresses someone's thoughts or beliefs. Label the statements F for *fact* and O for *opinion*.

   _____ a. The Ark of the Covenant disappeared.

   _____ b. Ethiopia has a small population of Jews.

   _____ c. The legend of the Ark's location is fascinating.

3. **Keeping Events in Order**

Label the statements below 1, 2, and 3 to show the order in which the events happened.

_____ a. The Hebrews carried the Ark of the Covenant out of Egypt.

_____ b. The Ark disappeared from King Solomon's temple.

_____ c. Ethiopians claim that the Ark is in their country.

4. **Making Correct Inferences**

Two of the statements below are correct *inferences*, or reasonable guesses. They are based on information in the passage. The other statement is an incorrect, or faulty, inference. Label the statements C for *correct* inference and F for *faulty* inference.

_____ a. The lost Ark may actually exist.

_____ b. The traditions of Ethiopian Jews have a long tradition.

_____ c. The lost Ark is in Ethiopia.

5. **Understanding Main Ideas**

One of the statements below expresses the main idea of the passage. One statement is too general, or too broad. The other explains only part of the passage; it is too narrow. Label the statements M for *main idea,* B for *too broad,* and N for *too narrow.*

_____ a. Ethiopia has legends about the lost Ark.

_____ b. Faithful Jews may have traveled to Ethiopia, taking the Ark with them.

_____ c. Scholars have reason to believe that the Ethiopian legend of the lost Ark might be true.

Correct Answers, Part A _____

Correct Answers, Part B _____

Total Correct Answers _____

# The Father of Sherlock Holmes

A British physician who turned to writing, Arthur Conan Doyle thought he would be remembered for his historical novels. His fame, however, rests on his creation of the master detective of fiction, the incomparable Sherlock Holmes.

Arthur Conan Doyle was born in Edinburgh, Scotland, on May 22, 1859. He was the oldest son of Charles Doyle, a civil servant. His parents were Irish Roman Catholics, and he received his early education in a Jesuit school, Stonyhurst. Later he earned a medical degree at Edinburgh University. He started practice as a family physician in Southsea, England. His income was small, so he began writing stories to make ends meet. In 1891, he gave up medicine to concentrate on his writing.

Doyle was knighted in 1902 for his pamphlet justifying England's part in the Boer War, in which he served at a field hospital. He was married twice. The death of his son Kingsley in World War I intensified his interest in psychic phenomena, and in later years, he wrote and lectured on spiritualism. He died in Sussex, England, on July 7, 1930.

*A Study in Scarlet,* published in 1887, introduced Sherlock Holmes and his friend Dr. John Watson. The second Holmes story was *The Sign of Four.* In 1891, Doyle began a series for *Strand Magazine* called *The Adventures of Sherlock Holmes.*

Sherlock Holmes has become known to movie and television audiences as a tall, lean, pipe-smoking, violin-playing detective. He lived at 221B Baker Street in London, where he was often visited by Watson, an associate in his many adventures. According to Doyle, it was Watson who recorded the Sherlock Holmes stories for posterity.

Doyle said he modeled Holmes after one of his teachers in Edinburgh, Dr. Joseph Bell. Bell could, for example, glance at a corpse on the anatomy table and deduce that the person had been a left-handed shoemaker. "It is all very well to say that a man is clever," Doyle wrote, "but the reader wants to see examples of it—such examples as Bell gave us every day in the wards." The author eventually became bored with Holmes and arranged for Holmes to be killed off in one of his stories. In response to readers' protests, Doyle wrote his next story explaining how the detective had miraculously survived the death struggle on the edge of a precipice. Doyle continued to write many stories about Holmes's exploits.

**Reading Time** _____

## Recalling Facts

1. Sherlock Holmes was modeled after
   - ❏ a. Arthur Conan Doyle.
   - ❏ b. Doyle's teacher.
   - ❏ c. Dr. John Watson.

2. Before he became a writer, Arthur Conan Doyle was a
   - ❏ a. soldier.
   - ❏ b. spiritualist.
   - ❏ c. physician.

3. Arthur Conan Doyle became a writer because
   - ❏ a. he needed the money.
   - ❏ b. good writers were scarce.
   - ❏ c. his parents encouraged him to do so.

4. Sherlock Holmes is a
   - ❏ a. fictional detective.
   - ❏ b. real person.
   - ❏ c. famous writer.

5. The story that introduced Holmes and Watson is titled
   - ❏ a. *The Adventures of Sherlock Holmes.*
   - ❏ b. *A Study in Scarlet.*
   - ❏ c. *The Sign of Four.*

## Understanding Ideas

6. Readers protested Holmes's death, which suggests that
   - ❏ a. Holmes was very popular.
   - ❏ b. readers wanted Doyle to write about a different character.
   - ❏ c. Doyle was bored with Holmes.

7. You can conclude from the article that Doyle admired Joseph Bell because Bell was
   - ❏ a. Doyle's teacher.
   - ❏ b. clever.
   - ❏ c. a good writer.

8. Doyle's pamphlet about Britain's role in the Boer War suggests that he was
   - ❏ a. patriotic.
   - ❏ b. against war.
   - ❏ c. unconcerned about national events.

9. The article suggests that Doyle
   - ❏ a. cared about his reading audience.
   - ❏ b. was not influenced by readers' concerns.
   - ❏ c. was critical of fans of Sherlock Holmes.

10. You can conclude from the article that Doyle's writings
    - ❏ a. were mostly historical novels.
    - ❏ b. included fiction and nonfiction.
    - ❏ c. were based on his medical career.

# 7　B　　Doyle to the Rescue

As famous as his fictional detective, Sherlock Holmes, Sir Arthur Conan Doyle also tried his hand at detective work. At least once, he agreed to use Holmes's methods of deduction in an actual criminal case.

The defendant in the case had been accused of killing some livestock in a field. Although the evidence against him was not particularly strong and he protested his innocence, the defendant was tried, convicted, and sentenced to prison. Released after three years, he petitioned for a pardon, citing evidence that he had not committed the crime. However, the court felt that the evidence was not conclusive and refused the pardon.

The defendant asked Sir Arthur Conan Doyle for help. Doyle studied the evidence and made the observation that the shoes worn by the convicted man on the day of the crime were stained with black mud. Mud in the field where the livestock had been killed was of yellow, sandy clay. Added to the other evidence of the man's innocence, Doyle's observation led to a full pardon.

The case became famous in England because of Doyle's participation. Eventually, resolution of this case changed the English court system by leading to the establishment of a formal court of appeals.

1. **Recognizing Words in Context**

   Find the word *citing* in the passage. One definition below is a *synonym* for that word; it means the same or almost the same thing. One definition is an *antonym*; it has the opposite or nearly opposite meaning. The other has a completely different meaning. Label the definitions S for *synonym*, A for *antonym*, and D for *different*.

   _____ a. seeing

   _____ b. quoting

   _____ c. ignoring

2. **Distinguishing Fact from Opinion**

   Two of the statements below present *facts*, which can be proved correct. The other statement is an *opinion*, which expresses someone's thoughts or beliefs. Label the statements F for *fact* and O for *opinion*.

   _____ a. Doyle observed that the mud on the man's shoes was black.

   _____ b. Doyle was as famous as his creation, Holmes.

   _____ c. Doyle agreed to help in a real criminal case.

## 3. Keeping Events in Order

Label the statements below 1, 2, and 3 to show the order in which the events happened.

\_\_\_\_\_ a. Doyle contributed his observations to the evidence.

\_\_\_\_\_ b. The defendant received a pardon.

\_\_\_\_\_ c. The defendant was tried and convicted.

## 4. Making Correct Inferences

Two of the statements below are correct *inferences*, or reasonable guesses. They are based on information in the passage. The other statement is an incorrect, or faulty, inference. Label the statements C for *correct* inference and F for *faulty* inference.

\_\_\_\_\_ a. Accurate observation plays an important role in justice.

\_\_\_\_\_ b. Doyle was solely responsible for the defendant's release.

\_\_\_\_\_ c. Doyle indirectly contributed to a change in the English justice system.

## 5. Understanding Main Ideas

One of the statements below expresses the main idea of the passage. One statement is too general, or too broad. The other explains only part of the passage; it is too narrow. Label the statements M for *main idea*, B for *too broad*, and N for *too narrow*.

\_\_\_\_\_ a. Accurate observation solves mysteries.

\_\_\_\_\_ b. At least once, Sir Arthur Conan Doyle proved Sherlock Holmes's methods by using them in a real court case.

\_\_\_\_\_ c. Doyle observed that the mud on the defendant's shoes was different from the mud in the field.

Correct Answers, Part A \_\_\_\_\_

Correct Answers, Part B \_\_\_\_\_

Total Correct Answers \_\_\_\_\_

　　　　# Miraculous Organ

The human brain is a miraculous organ. It has many functions. The brain regulates thought, memory, judgment, personal identity, and other aspects of what is commonly called mind. It also regulates many other aspects of the human body, including body temperature, blood pressure, and the activity of internal organs. All of these brain activities help the body respond to its environment and to maintain sound health. In fact, the brain is considered so central to human well-being and survival that the death of the brain is considered in many parts of the world to be the legal test to determine whether a person has died.

The brain is generally defined as the part of the central nervous system that is contained in the skull. The rest of the central nervous system consists of an elongated tube of nerve tissue called the spinal cord. The spinal cord extends from the base of the brain and is contained within the bony vertebral canal. The brain controls the activities of the body and receives information about the body's inner workings and about the outside world by sending and receiving signals via the spinal cord and the peripheral nervous system. The brain receives the oxygen and food it needs to function through a vast network of arteries. The arteries carry fresh blood to every part of the brain.

The brain of a human adult weighs about three pounds (1.35 kilograms). It looks like a mushroom contained within the skull. The cap of the mushroom—the very top of the brain—is the cerebrum. The stem of the mushroom is that part of the brain that is attached to the spinal cord. This is called the medulla oblongata, or brain stem. At the back of the head, lying between the brain stem and the cerebrum, is the area known as the cerebellum.

Generally, the lower a part of the brain is within the skull, the more primitive and basic its function is. Also, the less likely it is that conscious control is involved in regulating the function. Thus the brain stem, the lowest part of the brain, is involved with the most basic processes, such as relaying information between parts of the brain or between the brain and the body to regulate basic body functions. The cerebellum controls balance and coordination. The cerebrum, the topmost part of the brain, is the "thinking" part of the brain.

**Reading Time** _____

## Recalling Facts

1. The legal test of death in many countries is when
   - ❏ a. the heart stops.
   - ❏ b. the brain dies.
   - ❏ c. breathing stops.

2. The brain is part of the
   - ❏ a. spinal cord.
   - ❏ b. peripheral nervous system.
   - ❏ c. central nervous system.

3. The brain of a human adult weighs about
   - ❏ a. one pound (0.45 kilograms).
   - ❏ b. two pounds (0.90 kilograms).
   - ❏ c. three pounds (1.35 kilograms).

4. The thinking part of the brain is called the
   - ❏ a. cerebellum.
   - ❏ b. cerebrum.
   - ❏ c. medulla oblongata.

5. The brain stem is involved with
   - ❏ a. balance and coordination.
   - ❏ b. thinking.
   - ❏ c. relaying information.

## Understanding Ideas

6. You can conclude from the article that the brain
   - ❏ a. is independent of the rest of the body.
   - ❏ b. survives without food.
   - ❏ c. depends on arteries to survive.

7. The part of the brain that controls breathing is the
   - ❏ a. cerebrum.
   - ❏ b. brain stem.
   - ❏ c. nerves.

8. The part of the brain that controls decision making is the
   - ❏ a. cerebrum.
   - ❏ b. cerebellum.
   - ❏ c. nerves.

9. The brain, spinal cord, and peripheral nervous system could be compared to
   - ❏ a. a communications network.
   - ❏ b. a book.
   - ❏ c. a tennis match.

10. The article wants you to understand that the human brain
    - ❏ a. regulates personality and function.
    - ❏ b. is more important than the heart.
    - ❏ c. can be compared to the brain of an animal.

# 8 B How We See

One function of the brain is to translate visual information into sight. Visual information reaches the eye as rays of light bouncing off the objects around us. The light waves enter the eye through the lens and form an upside-down image on the back of the eye, the retina.

The retina has more than 125 million structures called rods and cones that translate the rays of light into strings of nerve impulses. These impulses communicate information about pattern, shape, size, and color to the optic nerve, which carries the information to the brain.

Inside the brain, the long fibers of the optic nerve extend from each eye to both the right and left sides of the brain, so visual information reaches both sides at the same time. From there, it travels to different visual areas in the brain that analyze the information. The brain also reconciles the slightly different images we see with each eye and compares the visual information with what we already know. All of this happens so fast that we experience the image in the same instant that we look at it, one of the true miracles of brain function.

## 1. Recognizing Words in Context

Find the word *reconciles* in the passage. One definition below is a *synonym* for that word; it means the same or almost the same thing. One definition is an *antonym;* it has the opposite or nearly opposite meaning. The other has a completely different meaning. Label the definitions *S* for *synonym*, A for *antonym*, and D for *different*.

\_\_\_\_\_ a. ignores

\_\_\_\_\_ b. adjusts

\_\_\_\_\_ c. repeats

## 2. Distinguishing Fact from Opinion

Two of the statements below present *facts,* which can be proved correct. The other statement is an *opinion,* which expresses someone's thoughts or beliefs. Label the statements F for *fact* and O for *opinion.*

\_\_\_\_\_ a. Visual images enter the eye through the lens.

\_\_\_\_\_ b. The retina has more than 125 million rods and cones.

\_\_\_\_\_ c. Vision is a true miracle of brain function.

## 3. Keeping Events in Order

Label the statements below 1, 2, and 3 to show the order in which the events happened.

_____ a. The rods and cones translate the light rays into nerve impulses.

_____ b. The optic nerve carries information to the brain.

_____ c. Visual information enters the eye as light rays.

## 4. Making Correct Inferences

Two of the statements below are correct *inferences,* or reasonable guesses. They are based on information in the passage. The other statement is an incorrect, or faulty, inference. Label the statements C for *correct* inference and F for *faulty* inference.

_____ a. Vision is a very complex process.

_____ b. Visual processes are easy to study.

_____ c. The retina is important to vision.

## 5. Understanding Main Ideas

One of the statements below expresses the main idea of the passage. One statement is too general, or too broad. The other explains only part of the passage; it is too narrow. Label the statements M for *main idea,* B for *too broad,* and N for *too narrow.*

_____ a. The complex process of vision is one of the brain's most marvelous activities.

_____ b. The retina, with 125 million rods and cones, translates light into nerve impulses.

_____ c. The brain helps us see.

Correct Answers, Part A _____

Correct Answers, Part B _____

Total Correct Answers _____

# A Strong Government

Soon after the United States had won the Revolutionary War, different groups within the country became discontented. The government under the Articles of Confederation seemed weak. It could not control people at home or make the new republic respected abroad. The new government would have to be strong for the young nation to survive.

One difficulty faced by the new government was that Congress did not have power to raise money. It could only ask for money from the states. Consequently, it was always poor. Congress also had no authority to regulate commerce. Some states began laying tariffs and other burdens on the shipping trade of their neighbors. This caused problems.

All states were supposed to abide by the Articles of Confederation; yet some states did not. They made treaties with the Indians and agreements with each other. They ignored foreign treaties made by Congress and regulated the value of money.

By 1785, many patriotic citizens thought that the government set up by the Articles of Confederation was a failure. George Washington, Alexander Hamilton, John Jay, James Madison, and other leaders repeatedly declared that the government should be strengthened. Some Americans had special reasons for wanting a stronger government. One group was made up of westerners who after the American Revolution had moved into Kentucky, Tennessee, and the new Northwest Territory. These westerners wanted a powerful federal government to protect them from the Indians, the Spaniards, and the British. Others who speculated in western lands believed that a strong national government would make these lands more valuable.

Another group who wanted a stronger government was made up of merchants, traders, and shipowners who suffered from tariff wars among the states and from injurious British laws. In addition, people who had lent money to the government during the war or just after it felt that a stronger government would be more likely to repay them.

Perhaps the most important group was made up of well-to-do businesspeople who owned mortgages and notes. They wanted a strong national government to take complete control of the currency and to prevent any state laws impairing the obligation of contracts.

The United States Constitution was written in response to the need for a stronger government. It is the oldest written constitution among the major nations of the world and the first to limit the powers that the federal government can exercise over its citizens.

**Reading Time** _____

## Recalling Facts

1. After the Revolutionary War, Congress faced
   - ❏ a. a bright future.
   - ❏ b. high taxes.
   - ❏ c. a lack of money.

2. The Articles of Confederation applied to
   - ❏ a. all the states.
   - ❏ b. five states.
   - ❏ c. states engaged in trade.

3. According to the Articles of Confederation, Congress had no authority to
   - ❏ a. repay loans.
   - ❏ b. make treaties.
   - ❏ c. regulate commerce.

4. A problem facing the state of Kentucky was
   - ❏ a. inexpensive land.
   - ❏ b. Indian control.
   - ❏ c. tariff wars.

5. The United States Constitution was the first
   - ❏ a. to limit the powers of the federal government.
   - ❏ b. to declare war.
   - ❏ c. system of government used after the Revolution.

## Understanding Ideas

6. The article suggests that
   - ❏ a. a strong federal government is better than a weak one.
   - ❏ b. state laws should overpower those of the federal government.
   - ❏ c. a weak federal government makes for a better-managed country.

7. You can conclude from the article that most groups wanting a stronger government
   - ❏ a. had the good of the country in mind.
   - ❏ b. were influenced by their own special interests.
   - ❏ c. had little influence on the government.

8. Of the issues facing the new government, the most crucial was
   - ❏ a. Indian control.
   - ❏ b. lack of money.
   - ❏ c. foreign trade.

9. You can conclude from the article that to solve the problems facing the country, the new federal government
   - ❏ a. was given more power.
   - ❏ b. was disbanded.
   - ❏ c. gave more power to the states.

10. It is likely that in limiting the powers of the federal government, the aim of the Constitution was to
    - ❏ a. protect the freedom of its citizens.
    - ❏ b. ensure the failure of the government.
    - ❏ c. win respect abroad.

# Our Bill of Rights

In May of 1787, all hopes for the future of the United States of America were centered on a group of delegates meeting in Philadelphia. Their purpose was to draft a constitution that would strengthen the young country and unite it. The Constitution they wrote, however, started a major battle when it was sent to the states to be ratified.

The new nation became divided between the Federalists, who supported the Constitution, and the Antifederalists, who opposed strong national control. The Antifederalists demanded that a bill of rights be added to the Constitution to protect the rights of the people.

At first, James Madison sided with the Federalists. He claimed, "The truth is . . . that the Constitution is itself, in every rational sense, and to every useful purpose, A BILL OF RIGHTS." He soon came to support the idea of a bill of rights, however. Madison drafted a list of amendments to the Constitution, which he presented to Congress in 1789. With some changes, Madison's list became the first ten amendments to the Constitution. These amendments are also known as the Bill of Rights. The demands of the people had supplied the missing piece of the United States Constitution.

1. **Recognizing Words in Context**

   Find the word *centered* in the passage. One definition below is a *synonym* for that word; it means the same or almost the same thing. One definition is an *antonym;* it has the opposite or nearly opposite meaning. The other has a completely different meaning. Label the definitions *S* for *synonym*, A for *antonym*, and D for *different*.

   _____ a. amidst

   _____ b. focused

   _____ c. deflected

2. **Distinguishing Fact from Opinion**

   Two of the statements below present *facts,* which can be proved correct. The other statement is an *opinion,* which expresses someone's thoughts or beliefs. Label the statements F for *fact* and O for *opinion.*

   _____ a. The Antifederalists were opposed to the Constitution.

   _____ b. A bill of rights was not necessary.

   _____ c. James Madison changed his mind about the need for a bill of rights.

## 3. Keeping Events in Order

Two of the statements below describe events that happened at the same time. The other statement describes an event that happened before or after those events. Label them S for *same time,* B for *before,* and A for *after.*

_____ a. James Madison drafted a bill of rights for the Constitution.

_____ b. A group of delegates met in Philadelphia in 1787.

_____ c. The convention drafted a new constitution for the United States.

## 4. Making Correct Inferences

Two of the statements below are correct *inferences,* or reasonable guesses. They are based on information in the passage. The other statement is an incorrect, or faulty, inference. Label the statements C for *correct* inference and F for *faulty* inference.

_____ a. James Madison had not really believed what he said about the Constitution being in itself a bill of rights.

_____ b. Without the Bill of Rights, the Constitution did not truly protect the rights of the people.

_____ c. The Federalists felt that the Constitution was protection enough without a bill of rights.

## 5. Understanding Main Ideas

One of the statements below expresses the main idea of the passage. One statement is too general, or too broad. The other explains only part of the passage; it is too narrow. Label the statements M for *main idea,* B for *too broad,* and N for *too narrow.*

_____ a. The Bill of Rights was drafted and added to the United States Constitution.

_____ b. The strengthening of the federal government began with the Constitutional Convention of 1787.

_____ c. The Antifederalists opposed strong national control.

Correct Answers, Part A _____

Correct Answers, Part B _____

Total Correct Answers _____

Sculpture and painting are both art, but sculpture differs from painting in a significant respect. A painting is flat and can show only the view taken by the painter. Sculpture, though, can be seen from many angles. Consequently, a sculptor strives to create perfect sculpture from every angle. A sculptor's goal is to achieve sense and rhythm for every possible point of view. To fashion sculpture, artists learned to use certain materials and to develop appropriate tools and processes.

Clay has been used for ceramics and sculpture since earliest times. Baked clay, known as terra cotta, can be glazed and unglazed. Terra cotta was used with great artistry by early peoples. Many terra cotta pieces have been unearthed at the sites of ancient cities and towns.

Carving is the process of reducing substances such as stone, wood, or ivory to a desired shape by cutting or chipping away unnecessary parts. The earliest carvings were probably nothing more than figures scratched into the flat surface of a rock. As time went on, primitive sculptors discovered that cutting away the background surrounding a figure made the figure appear more real.

Carving requires a sure knowledge of the final form. Material such as marble or granite cannot be restored once it is cut off. To lessen the risk of error, sculptors often make small models in clay, wax, or plasticine. Modeling is the process of manipulating these materials into the desired shape. A model is scaled to proper proportions before the sculptor undertakes the final carving.

Sometimes a pointing machine is used to help transfer the exact contours of a model to the final stone. This machine, which uses a moving needle, transfers to the final material a series of points corresponding exactly to those made on the model. With this mechanical guide the sculptor knows just where to carve.

Until about the end of the Renaissance in Italy, sculptors did their own final cutting in the stone. Today, many master sculptors work out a detailed scale model alone. Then they turn over the final work to trained studio assistants and expert stonecutters.

The sculpture of Egypt, Mesopotamia, Greece, China, and Europe of the Middle Ages was generally given a painted surface, known as polychromy. First a thin coat of plaster (gesso) was applied over the wood or stone. Then the works were painted bright colors to help give a greater sense of realism.

**Reading Time** _____

## Recalling Facts

1. Cutting or chipping away unnecessary parts is called
   - ❏ a. plasticine.
   - ❏ b. modeling.
   - ❏ c. carving.

2. Terra cotta is
   - ❏ a. baked clay.
   - ❏ b. uncarved marble.
   - ❏ c. plasticine.

3. The process of manipulating plastic materials is called
   - ❏ a. molding.
   - ❏ b. modeling.
   - ❏ c. glazing.

4. To lessen the risk for error, carvers
   - ❏ a. make models.
   - ❏ b. carve directly on granite.
   - ❏ c. work with assistants.

5. Pointing machines act as
   - ❏ a. sculptors' models.
   - ❏ b. cutting tools.
   - ❏ c. mechanical guides.

## Understanding Ideas

6. The term *three-dimensional* can be applied to
   - ❏ a. paintings and sculpture.
   - ❏ b. sculpture.
   - ❏ c. painting.

7. Primitive peoples created sculptures out of terra cotta, which suggests that
   - ❏ a. they were skilled artisans.
   - ❏ b. clay was scarce.
   - ❏ c. they did not use other materials.

8. The article suggests that carving
   - ❏ a. is an intricate process.
   - ❏ b. was used mainly by primitive peoples.
   - ❏ c. requires little skill.

9. You can conclude from the article that people of the Middle Ages
   - ❏ a. were against artistic expression.
   - ❏ b. preferred colorful art.
   - ❏ c. did not like realistic art.

10. Carving with the help of a pointing machine
   - ❏ a. takes away from the artistry of a finished sculpture.
   - ❏ b. makes a finished sculpture less realistic.
   - ❏ c. is an example of blending technology with art.

## 10 B     Gift from the Sea

"What a great vacation it's been so far!" Trisha exclaimed to Paul as the two of them checked their scuba gear and headed into the Mediterranean Sea.

The blue-green waters off the coast of southern Italy were crystal clear as they swam out. About 300 yards (270 meters) from shore, Trisha spotted something on the ocean bottom; she tapped Paul's shoulder and pointed. Their eyes widened in wonder as they peered at what they had found. Rising from the sandy floor of the ocean was a hand attached to a muscular forearm! Pushing deeper, the divers hovered over the arm and tentatively touched its bronze surface. They wondered what might be attached to the beckoning arm. Tugging at it, they realized it was too heavy to budge. Paul pointed landward, and back they sped.

A few days later, they stood on the beach and watched as a boat equipped with a crane lifted the ancient statue from its watery grave. "How old do you think it is, professor?" Trisha asked the archaeologist supervising the procedure. "How do you think it got there?"

"Oh, it's about twenty-four centuries old, I suspect," he answered. "A Roman ship returning from Greece may have been caught in a storm. It probably sank somewhere near here. This is quite a valuable find, my friends."

"And this has been quite a vacation!" Paul said.

1. **Recognizing Words in Context**

   Find the word *spotted* in the passage. One definition below is a *synonym* for that word; it means the same or almost the same thing. One definition is an *antonym;* it has the opposite or nearly opposite meaning. The other has a completely different meaning. Label the definitions *S* for *synonym,* A for *antonym,* and D for *different.*

   _____ a. overlooked

   _____ b. dotted

   _____ c. saw

2. **Distinguishing Fact from Opinion**

   Two of the statements below present *facts,* which can be proved correct. The other statement is an *opinion,* which expresses someone's thoughts or beliefs. Label the statements F for *fact* and O for *opinion.*

   _____ a. A Roman ship had probably sunk while returning from Greece.

   _____ b. While scuba diving, Trisha and Paul found an ancient statue.

   _____ c. Trisha and Paul were vacationing in Italy.

## 3. Keeping Events in Order

Label the statements below 1, 2, and 3 to show the order in which the events happened.

_____ a. Trisha and Paul swam back to shore.

_____ b. A crane lifted the statue from the ocean.

_____ c. They saw a hand attached to a muscular forearm rising out of the sand.

## 4. Making Correct Inferences

Two of the statements below are correct *inferences*, or reasonable guesses. They are based on information in the passage. The other statement is an incorrect, or faulty, inference. Label the statements C for *correct* inference and F for *faulty* inference.

_____ a. Trisha and Paul reported their find to an archaeologist.

_____ b. Trisha and Paul knew that they had made an important discovery.

_____ c. Trisha and Paul were going to receive a lot of money for their find.

## 5. Understanding Main Ideas

One of the statements below expresses the main idea of the passage. One statement is too general, or too broad. The other explains only part of the passage; it is too narrow. Label the statements M for *main idea*, B for *too broad*, and N for *too narrow*.

_____ a. An archaeologist believed the statue was about twenty-four centuries old.

_____ b. While scuba diving, two vacationers found an ancient statue on the ocean floor.

_____ c. Many treasures lie hidden beneath the ocean depths.

Correct Answers, Part A  _____

Correct Answers, Part B  _____

Total Correct Answers  _____

# No Fun in the Sun

Remember how much sunburn hurt when you were a child? Sunburn still hurts, but long-term damage from the sun may be worse. Medical experts believe that too much exposure to the sun as children and teenagers is a major cause of skin cancer, increasingly common in this country, and premature skin aging in adults. Regular sun exposure throughout the year as adults also contributes to long-term skin damage. Even people with darker complexions, who have more natural protection against the sun, are at risk. Two kinds of ultraviolet sun rays, UVA and UVB, can cause skin damage. This damage can range from immediate effects such as burning, photosensitive reactions (rashes), cell damage, and tissue damage to long-term consequences such as wrinkling and skin cancer.

People who work outside—lifeguards, letter carriers, gardeners, and construction workers, for example—may be at even higher risk for skin damage. These workers like everyone else, including children and teenagers, need adequate protection before going out in the sun.

You can protect your skin from damage by taking the right steps early. Always use sunscreens. Many dermatologists believe that children and teenagers who regularly use sunscreens can significantly reduce the risk of skin damage later in life. Use waterproof or water-resistant sunscreens that help protect skin from both UVA and UVB rays and have SPF (sun protection factor) numbers of at least 15. Apply sunscreen liberally (at least one large handful for a body) about 30 minutes before going outside. No matter what sunscreen product is used, reapply it after swimming or perspiring heavily. Be aware that no sunscreen totally blocks the sun's harmful rays. Even people wearing high SPF sunscreens get some exposure to ultraviolet rays.

There are some other important measures you can take. Avoid scheduling outdoor activities when the sun is strongest, from 10:00 A.M. to 3:00 P.M. When you do go out in the sun, dress for maximum protection. Wear hats with brims and long-sleeved shirts and pants that are tightly weaved. They offer the best protection. Sunglasses help to protect the eyes. Select sunglasses that help to screen out both UVA and UVB rays; UV rays may contribute to the development of cataracts. Sunglasses that are close fitting to the face and have larger lenses offer more protection.

Lastly, avoid going to tanning parlors. Skin-care specialists claim that tanning devices can damage the skin and eyes as much as direct sunlight.

**Reading Time** _____

## Recalling Facts

1. Sunscreens should have a sun protection factor (SPF) of at least
   - ❑ a. 10.
   - ❑ b. 15.
   - ❑ c. 20.

2. The sun is strongest in
   - ❑ a. early morning.
   - ❑ b. midday.
   - ❑ c. late afternoon.

3. Wearing sunglasses may help prevent
   - ❑ a. cataracts.
   - ❑ b. photosensitive reactions.
   - ❑ c. premature aging.

4. Skin-care specialists claim that tanning devices
   - ❑ a. are not harmful.
   - ❑ b. can cause as much damage as the sun's rays.
   - ❑ c. are less damaging than direct sunlight.

5. A group of people that the article identifies as being at higher risk from sun exposure are
   - ❑ a. construction workers.
   - ❑ b. teenagers.
   - ❑ c. dermatologists.

## Understanding Ideas

6. The article wants you to recognize that people
   - ❑ a. can endanger themselves by getting too much sun.
   - ❑ b. are better off staying indoors.
   - ❑ c. should spend more time in the shade.

7. The damaging effects of the sun show up
   - ❑ a. during the teenage years.
   - ❑ b. later in life.
   - ❑ c. under ultraviolet light.

8. What does the article imply regarding skin cancer?
   - ❑ a. It may be a preventable disease.
   - ❑ b. Sun exposure is not the cause of skin cancer.
   - ❑ c. The cure rate is encouraging.

9. Sunscreen should be reapplied after swimming, which suggests that
   - ❑ a. applying it before swimming doesn't work.
   - ❑ b. swimmers get too much sun.
   - ❑ c. water weakens its effectiveness.

10. Why do sunglasses with larger lenses offer more protection?
   - ❑ a. Larger lenses are more expensive and better made.
   - ❑ b. Larger lenses shield a larger area.
   - ❑ c. Larger lenses soak up more sun.

# A Better Idea

"Let's go to the beach today," Nita said as she looked out the window at the sun shining in a cloudless sky.

"Great suggestion," Rob said. Everyone agreed it was a perfect day for beach-going, and they started planning the excursion.

"Wait a minute," said Laurie. "Aren't you forgetting what we learned in health class this week about the dangers of ultraviolet rays? Getting a sunburn is bad enough, but I don't want to damage my skin so that I get skin cancer when I'm older. I don't want to get wrinkles early, either."

"Relax, Laurie. We'll wear sunscreen—SPF 30 or 45," said Phil.

"And sun block on our noses—that zinc oxide stuff that stays white," added Jen.

"We'll bring a beach umbrella," put in Rob, "and wear hats and bring long pants and long-sleeved shirts to put on when we get out of the water."

"And sunglasses," added Nita. "In addition to making you look fabulous, sunglasses can protect your eyes from UV rays."

"I think I have an alternative idea that might be just as much fun as going to the beach," said Laurie. "Instead, why don't we have a picnic in the shade on my back porch and then go for a swim at the YMCA? By staying out of the sun, we'll be totally safe from ultraviolet rays."

Everyone enthusiastically agreed that this was a superior idea.

## 1. Recognizing Words in Context

Find the word *perfect* in the passage. One definition below is a *synonym* for that word; it means the same or almost the same thing. One definition is an *antonym;* it has the opposite or nearly opposite meaning. The other has a completely different meaning. Label the definitions S for *synonym,* A for *antonym,* and D for *different.*

_____ a. sunny

_____ b. faulty

_____ c. flawless

## 2. Distinguishing Fact from Opinion

Two of the statements below present *facts,* which can be proved correct. The other statement is an *opinion,* which expresses someone's thoughts or beliefs. Label the statements F for *fact* and O for *opinion.*

_____ a. Sunglasses can protect your eyes from UV rays.

_____ b. By staying out of the sun, they would be totally safe from UV rays.

_____ c. It was a perfect day for beach-going.

3. **Keeping Events in Order**

Label the statements below 1, 2, and 3 to show the order in which the events happened.

_____ a. Laurie suggested a picnic in the shade and a swim at the YMCA.

_____ b. Laurie reminded the group about the dangers of ultraviolet rays.

_____ c. Nita suggested a day at the beach.

4. **Making Correct Inferences**

Two of the statements below are correct *inferences,* or reasonable guesses. They are based on information in the passage. The other statement is an incorrect, or faulty, inference. Label the statements C for *correct* inference and F for *faulty* inference.

_____ a. The young people in the group knew what they should do to protect themselves against ultraviolet rays.

_____ b. Everyone would have preferred to go to the beach.

_____ c. Everyone wanted to stay safe from UV rays.

5. **Understanding Main Ideas**

One of the statements below expresses the main idea of the passage. One statement is too general, or too broad. The other explains only part of the passage; it is too narrow. Label the statements M for *main idea,* B for *too broad,* and N for *too narrow.*

_____ a. The young people had learned about the dangers of ultraviolet rays in health class.

_____ b. The dangers of sunlight should be considered when making plans for an outing.

_____ c. Ultraviolet rays are harmful.

Correct Answers, Part A _____

Correct Answers, Part B _____

Total Correct Answers _____

# 12 A    Shortened Words

A shortened form of a word or group of words used in writing to save time and space is called an abbreviation. Some abbreviations are also used in speaking.

Abbreviations often consist of the first letter of a word, or of each important word in a group, written as a capital letter. Sometimes abbreviations are followed by a period. For example, *P.O.* stands for post office and *C.O.D.* for collect (or cash) on delivery.

Sometimes an abbreviation is a small letter that may or may not be followed by a period. Examples include *b.* for born and *d.* for died. The same abbreviation may be used for different words. For example, *m.* may stand for married, masculine, and meter. When an abbreviation can be used for more than one word, the reader can use context to determine its meaning.

Sometimes abbreviations are made up of more than one letter of a word. Examples include *ms.* for manuscript and *ft* for foot. Some abbreviations form a new word, as with *NATO* (North Atlantic Treaty Organization) and *OPEC* (Organization of Petroleum Exporting Countries). Such abbreviations are called acronyms. Letters in abbreviations may be doubled for the plural form, as in *ll.* for lines and *pp.* for pages. For certain frequently used abbreviations, small capital letters are usually used, as in *A.D., B.C., A.M.,* and *P.M.*

Abbreviations are often used for common words such as the names of days, months, and states. Abbreviations may be used for long words and phrases, for example, *Lieut.* for Lieutenant and *R.F.D.* for Rural Free Delivery. Academic degrees and titles are usually abbreviated, as in *D.D.* for Doctor of Divinity and *Dr.* for doctor. Businesses use *Co.* for Company, *Inc.* for Incorporated, and *Ltd.* for Limited.

Abbreviations for many Latin phrases in common use are made up of just the first letter of each word, as in *n.b.* for *nota bene* ("note well") and *i.e.* for *id est* ("that is"). An exception is *etc.* for *et cetera* ("and others").

Ancient monuments and manuscripts show that humans began to abbreviate words soon after alphabetic writing became general. In the United States, abbreviations have long been accepted. *OK* and *C.O.D.* date from the 19th century. Even agencies of the federal government are now commonly referred to by their initials. For example, *FHA,* for Federal Housing Administration, and *NASA,* for National Aeronautics and Space Administration, have become household words.

**Reading Time** _____

## Recalling Facts

1. Abbreviations are used in
   - ❏ a. writing only.
   - ❏ b. speaking only.
   - ❏ c. writing and speaking.

2. When the same abbreviation is used for different words, the meaning can be determined from
   - ❏ a. the dictionary.
   - ❏ b. the context.
   - ❏ c. capitalization.

3. Abbreviations for most Latin phrases are usually
   - ❏ a. acronyms.
   - ❏ b. the first two letters.
   - ❏ c. the first letter of each word.

4. Humans began to abbreviate words
   - ❏ a. soon after alphabetic writing became general.
   - ❏ b. before alphabetic writing became general.
   - ❏ c. in the 20th century.

5. The purpose of abbreviations is to
   - ❏ a. save time and space.
   - ❏ b. indicate when something was written.
   - ❏ c. confuse the reader or listener.

## Understanding Ideas

6. Words that are often abbreviated are probably
   - ❏ a. frequently used words.
   - ❏ b. uncommon words.
   - ❏ c. foreign words.

7. *WAC*, which stands for Women's Army Corps, is
   - ❏ a. a Latin phrase.
   - ❏ b. an acronym.
   - ❏ c. a plural abbreviation.

8. Abbreviations on ancient monuments were most likely used to
   - ❏ a. save time.
   - ❏ b. save space.
   - ❏ c. show off.

9. Long official names are increasingly referred to by their initials, which suggests that
   - ❏ a. people are getting lazier.
   - ❏ b. it is easier and quicker to refer to initials.
   - ❏ c. long names are becoming obsolete.

10. The decision to change state abbreviations, such as *Mass.* to *MA,* was most likely due to a
    - ❏ a. desire to simplify mailing addresses.
    - ❏ b. decrease in the size of envelopes.
    - ❏ c. post office error.

# For Short

Ms. Talbot, the language arts teacher, asked the class to analyze the abbreviations used in the newspaper's classified ads. Brian and Leah are reading apartment ads, while Talia and Aaron are puzzling over the personals.

"Listen to this advertisement," Brian said. "'Lg 2BR, yd, mod K&B, D&D, W/W, ht/hw, AC, $1,200 mo.' Makes you want to run right out and rent it, doesn't it?"

"Sure," responded Leah, "if I knew what it all meant. *D&D*, what could that possibly mean? Dreary and drab? And what's *W/W*? Windows and walls? Aren't those a given?"

"I know that *W/W* means wall-to-wall carpeting and *AC* is air conditioning. But I don't know what the other abbreviations mean," Brian replied.

"Hey, Talia, have you finished deciphering your ad?" Brian asked.

"Ha!" Talia exclaimed. "Aaron and I have a real puzzler."

"She's absolutely right," responded Aaron. "'SM, N/S, N/D, seeks SF for friendship, poss LTR.' What does it mean?"

"Well, I know *SM* stands for single male and *SF* means single female, but after that, I'm clueless," moaned Talia.

"How can you ever rent an apartment or find a friend if you don't know what these cryptic abbreviations mean?" Brian asked.

"It's like trying to decode a secret message without having the key," explained Ms. Talbot. "Classified ads have a language of abbreviations all their own. Keep working at it!"

## 1. Recognizing Words in Context

Find the word *key* in the passage. One definition below is a *synonym* for that word; it means the same or almost the same thing. One definition is an *antonym;* it has the opposite or nearly opposite meaning. The other has a completely different meaning. Label the definitions S for *synonym,* A for *antonym,* and D for *different.*

_____ a. opener

_____ b. question

_____ c. solution

## 2. Distinguishing Fact from Opinion

Two of the statements below present *facts,* which can be proved correct. The other statement is an *opinion,* which expresses someone's thoughts or beliefs. Label the statements F for *fact* and O for *opinion.*

_____ a. Some classified ads use abbreviations.

_____ b. W/W means wall-to-wall carpet.

_____ c. The abbreviations used in classified ads are needlessly confusing.

## 3. Keeping Events in Order

Two of the statements below describe events that happened at the same time. The other statement describes an event that happened before or after those events. Label them S for *same time,* B for *before,* and A for *after.*

_____ a. Brian was trying to figure out the abbreviations used in an apartment ad.

_____ b. Ms. Talbot explained that reading classified ads was like trying to decode a secret message.

_____ c. Leah was analyzing a personal ad.

## 4. Making Correct Inferences

Two of the statements below are correct *inferences,* or reasonable guesses. They are based on information in the passage. The other statement is an incorrect, or faulty, inference. Label the statements C for *correct* inference and F for *faulty* inference.

_____ a. To understand classified ads, the reader has to be familiar with the abbreviations used in them.

_____ b. Ms. Talbot thought that classified ads are easy to read.

_____ c. Leah and Brian were having difficulty interpreting the meanings of some abbreviations.

## 5. Understanding Main Ideas

One of the statements below expresses the main idea of the passage. One statement is too general, or too broad. The other explains only part of the passage; it is too narrow. Label the statements M for *main idea,* B for *too broad,* and N for *too narrow.*

_____ a. Classified ads have their own special language of abbreviations.

_____ b. Classified ads include apartment and personal ads.

_____ c. Brian knew that *AC* meant air conditioning.

Correct Answers, Part A _____

Correct Answers, Part B _____

Total Correct Answers _____

The word *crocodilian* refers to both the alligator and the crocodile. Crocodilians are predators that are active mostly at night. During the day, they often lie at the water's edge, sunning themselves. At night, they retreat to the water. They live solitary lives and establish individual territories. A resident animal roars loudly at the approach of an intruder.

Young crocodiles and alligators eat worms and insects. As they mature, they add frogs, tadpoles, and fishes to their diets. Older animals eat mostly small animals, but some have even occasionally attacked humans. Crocodilians capture water animals in their jaws. To catch land animals, they knock unsuspecting prey into the water with their long, powerful tails. Animals too large to be swallowed whole are either torn to pieces or are drowned and permitted to decay in burrows. These burrows, which are dug at or just above the waterline, can extend for many feet and eventually end in a den, or chamber. The alligators hibernate in these burrows during cold weather.

Crocodilians draw strong reactions from their human neighbors, who have worshipped, feared, hunted, and tamed them for thousands of years. Ancient Egyptians considered the crocodile a symbol of the gods. Crocodiles are still regarded as sacred by some groups in Pakistan.

Crocodiles and alligators have been hunted for many reasons. The protection of domestic animals and the safety of humans are two reasons. Crocodiles are more likely to attack than are alligators, although alligators will attack when cornered. Humans kill thousands of crocodilians every year for sport and for commercial uses. Their skins provide leather for handbags, luggage, shoes, and belts. Alligators and crocodiles have also become pets and zoo specimens. If kept in captivity from birth, some learn to recognize their keepers, to beg for food, and to permit petting. Also, alligators and crocodiles have been bred and raised on farms to be harvested like other livestock.

The unrestricted hunting of crocodilians has severely depleted their population. The Chinese alligator is now considered rare. The disappearance of the crocodiles from parts of Africa has had a clear effect on the ecosystem. It has resulted in an overabundance of catfish. This, in turn, has greatly diminished the supply of other fishes. The American alligator has been on the increase since the Endangered Species Act gave it protection. Other governments also have passed laws to prevent the extinction of alligators and crocodiles.

**Reading Time** _____

## Recalling Facts

1. The word *crocodilian* refers to
   - ❑ a. alligators and crocodiles.
   - ❑ b. alligators.
   - ❑ c. crocodiles.

2. Young crocodiles and alligators eat
   - ❑ a. fishes.
   - ❑ b. worms and insects.
   - ❑ c. plants.

3. The number of crocodiles and alligators
   - ❑ a. is on the increase.
   - ❑ b. has greatly decreased.
   - ❑ c. is in the millions.

4. Ancient Egyptians thought of the crocodile as
   - ❑ a. an annoying pest.
   - ❑ b. a pet.
   - ❑ c. a symbol of the gods.

5. The American alligator is considered
   - ❑ a. the most dangerous alligator.
   - ❑ b. an endangered species.
   - ❑ c. to no longer exist.

## Understanding Ideas

6. The greatest danger to crocodilians is from
   - ❑ a. starvation.
   - ❑ b. each other.
   - ❑ c. humans.

7. The article suggests that crocodilians
   - ❑ a. should be hunted only for food.
   - ❑ b. should not be hunted.
   - ❑ c. need protection.

8. The extinction of alligators and crocodiles would result in
   - ❑ a. an imbalance of the ecosystem.
   - ❑ b. the enactment of new laws.
   - ❑ c. a more equitable distribution of fish.

9. The skins of crocodilians make them
   - ❑ a. commercially valuable.
   - ❑ b. good animals for sport hunting.
   - ❑ c. excellent pets.

10. Crocodilians are bred and raised on farms so that
    - ❑ a. those in the wild can be protected.
    - ❑ b. they can be used for commercial purposes.
    - ❑ c. humans will feel safer.

## 13 | B | Saving the Alligator

When early settlers came to what is now the southern United States, they were greeted by what one Georgia traveler called "the ugliest creature that walks or crawls." The traveler was referring to the alligator. Not many settlers knew much about alligators. But what they found out, they didn't like. They set out to exterminate the beasts in any way they could. However, they also found that alligator hides made excellent leather. A busy trade in alligator hide began in the 1860s and continued well into the next century.

By the 1950s, it was becoming hard to find alligators in the wild. The reptiles were in danger from overhunting. Louisiana and Florida, the two states where alligator hunters had been most active, began protecting alligators as endangered. The federal government followed soon afterward.

In recent years, the alligator population has been recovering. Controlled alligator hunting by licensed hunters helps to keep the number of alligators in check. Official alligator catchers respond to complaints about alligators in swimming pools, backyards, and golf courses, and they take the offenders away. Alligators are dangerous animals, but people are finally beginning to learn how to live with these unusual native American beasts.

1. **Recognizing Words in Context**

   Find the word *exterminate* in the passage. One definition below is a *synonym* for that word; it means the same or almost the same thing. One definition is an *antonym*; it has the opposite or nearly opposite meaning. The other has a completely different meaning. Label the definitions S for *synonym*, A for *antonym*, and D for *different*.

   _____ a. establish

   _____ b. eliminate

   _____ c. exclude

2. **Distinguishing Fact from Opinion**

   Two of the statements below present *facts*, which can be proved correct. The other statement is an *opinion*, which expresses someone's thoughts or beliefs. Label the statements F for *fact* and O for *opinion*.

   _____ a. The alligator is the ugliest thing that walks or crawls.

   _____ b. Alligator hide can be made into leather.

   _____ c. Alligators are native to America.

## 3. Keeping Events in Order

Label the statements below 1, 2, and 3 to show the order in which the events happened.

_____ a. The alligator population is recovering.

_____ b. Alligators began to disappear from the wild.

_____ c. Early settlers found alligators in the South.

## 4. Making Correct Inferences

Two of the statements below are correct *inferences,* or reasonable guesses. They are based on information in the passage. The other statement is an incorrect, or faulty, inference. Label the statements C for *correct* inference and F for *faulty* inference.

_____ a. Alligators should be killed because they are dangerous.

_____ b. Saving the alligator is worthwhile.

_____ c. The efforts to save wild alligators are succeeding.

## 5. Understanding Main Ideas

One of the statements below expresses the main idea of the passage. One statement is too general, or too broad. The other explains only part of the passage; it is too narrow. Label the statements M for *main idea,* B for *too broad,* and N for *too narrow.*

_____ a. Alligators are found in the southern United States.

_____ b. Controlled alligator hunting helps keep the alligator population in check.

_____ c. The alligator population was almost wiped out by overhunting, but it is recovering.

Correct Answers, Part A _____

Correct Answers, Part B _____

Total Correct Answers _____

## 14　A　Problem Drinking

An overwhelming desire to drink alcohol is a disease called alcoholism. Alcohol is a drug; it causes harm. In the United States, alcoholism is the most widespread form of drug abuse. Alcoholism affects at least 5 million persons. About one-third of high school students in the United States are thought to be problem drinkers. Many may be alcoholics. Drunk drivers account for one-half of all fatal automobile accidents each year. Drinking is a leading cause of loss of income. Heavy drinkers display social and personal problems.

Alcoholism also creates many severe physical problems. More than three drinks a day over even a few weeks causes destructive changes in the liver. About 15 percent of heavy drinkers develop cirrhosis, a liver disease that can be fatal. Changes in the brain and nervous system result in hostile behavior, loss of mental sharpness, and poor judgment. One-third of the babies born to mothers who drink heavily have birth defects or retardation. This condition is called fetal alcohol syndrome. Some drugs, such as tranquilizers, when taken with alcohol can result in death.

It has long been thought that alcohol abuse resulted from a combination of psychological and social factors. Current scientific research suggests that a tendency to abuse alcohol runs in families. An inherited chemical defect could play a role. Researchers have discovered a rare gene, possibly one of several that may lead to alcoholism. This suggests that in some cases the disease may be inherited.

A family or individual with an alcohol problem is in serious trouble. The alcoholic's main goal is to get something to drink. The drinking usually continues until the victim is drunk. Family, work, and friends are of little concern when there is a need for alcohol. Drunkenness inhibits the alcoholic's control of normal behavior. It depresses the ability to perform even the simplest functions.

Alcoholics can be helped. Two absolute rules apply to their recovery. An alcoholic must accept the fact that there is a real problem and decide to stop drinking. Second, the patient must also realize that any form or quantity of alcohol is literally poison. Most treatment experts believe that an alcoholic can never take another drink. Alcoholism is a lifelong condition.

Since the late 1940s, Antabuse and other drugs have been used to prevent drinking. The drug causes a violent physical reaction when alcohol is consumed. Problem drinkers can and are being helped.

**Reading Time** _____

## Recalling Facts

1. In the United States, alcoholism affects
   - ❏ a. adults only.
   - ❏ b. at least 5 million persons.
   - ❏ c. most people.

2. One-half of all fatal automobile accidents each year are caused by
   - ❏ a. teenagers.
   - ❏ b. bad weather.
   - ❏ c. drunk drivers.

3. Scientific research suggests that alcohol abuse
   - ❏ a. runs in families.
   - ❏ b. is most frequent in rural areas.
   - ❏ c. leads to drug addiction.

4. Antabuse helps prevent drinking by
   - ❏ a. eliminating the desire to drink.
   - ❏ b. causing a violent physical reaction when alcohol is consumed.
   - ❏ c. inhibiting the alcoholic's mental function.

5. Alcohol abuse causes cirrhosis, or damage to the
   - ❏ a. nervous system.
   - ❏ b. brain.
   - ❏ c. liver.

## Understanding Ideas

6. The article suggests that recovery from alcoholism depends mainly on
   - ❏ a. whether the disease is inherited.
   - ❏ b. the alcoholic's decision to stop drinking.
   - ❏ c. resources available to the alcoholic.

7. You can conclude from the article that alcoholics
   - ❏ a. can limit their drinking.
   - ❏ b. suffer no physical harm from drinking.
   - ❏ c. can cause problems for families and friends.

8. You can conclude from the article that the effects of alcoholism
   - ❏ a. are primarily physical.
   - ❏ b. include physical, economic, and social problems.
   - ❏ c. are not very important.

9. Alcoholism is the most widespread form of drug abuse in the United States, which suggests that
   - ❏ a. most Americans are problem drinkers.
   - ❏ b. Americans need to be better educated about the harmful effects of alcohol.
   - ❏ c. people in the United States should not be allowed to drink alcohol.

10. You can conclude from the article that causes of alcoholism are
    - ❏ a. well understood.
    - ❏ b. still being researched.
    - ❏ c. usually psychological.

# 14 B Alcoholics Anonymous

In 1935, Dr. Bob Smith and Bill Wilson founded Alcoholics Anonymous. This organization is a self-help support group for people who want to overcome problems with alcohol. "Keep it simple" were Smith's dying words to Wilson in 1950. True to Smith's wishes, AA has stuck to its simple formula to this day.

Smith and Wilson, both recovering alcoholics, realized that a good way for alcoholics to stay sober was to talk with other people who understood their problems. Alcoholics Anonymous offers support meetings at which members can turn to one another for help and advice. An AA member can find a meeting to attend almost anywhere in the world. AA's twelve-step approach—a kind of road map to recovery—has proved so successful that it has been adopted by other recovery programs, such as Overeaters Anonymous and Gamblers Anonymous.

There are also support groups for people involved in the lives of alcoholics. Al-Anon offers a support system for family members and friends of alcoholics. Alateen, an offshoot of Al-Anon, is for young people between the ages of twelve and twenty whose parents, other family members, or friends have drinking problems.

## 1. Recognizing Words in Context

Find the word *stuck* in the passage. One definition below is a *synonym* for that word; it means the same or almost the same thing. One definition is an *antonym;* it has the opposite or nearly opposite meaning. The other has a completely different meaning. Label the definitions S for *synonym,* A for *antonym,* and D for *different.*

_____ a. disregarded

_____ b. trapped

_____ c. adhered

## 2. Distinguishing Fact from Opinion

Two of the statements below present *facts,* which can be proved correct. The other statement is an *opinion,* which expresses someone's thoughts or beliefs. Label the statements F for *fact* and O for *opinion.*

_____ a. Smith and Wilson founded AA in 1935.

_____ b. Joining AA is the best way for an alcoholic to become and stay sober.

_____ c. AA takes a twelve-step approach to recovery.

3. **Keeping Events in Order**

Label the statements below 1, 2, and 3 to show the order in which the events happened.

_____ a. Smith told Wilson to "Keep it simple."

_____ b. Al-Anon was organized as support for families of alcoholics.

_____ c. Smith and Wilson founded Alcoholics Anonymous.

4. **Making Correct Inferences**

Two of the statements below are correct *inferences,* or reasonable guesses. They are based on information in the passage. The other statement is an incorrect, or faulty, inference. Label the statements C for *correct* inference and F for *faulty* inference.

_____ a. Smith and Wilson found a formula that worked for many alcoholics.

_____ b. People with alcoholic family members or friends also need support.

_____ c. All alcoholics would benefit from joining AA.

5. **Understanding Main Ideas**

One of the statements below expresses the main idea of the passage. One statement is too general, or too broad. The other explains only part of the passage; it is too narrow. Label the statements M for *main idea,* B for *too broad,* and N for *too narrow.*

_____ a. Alcoholics Anonymous was founded by Dr. Bob Smith and Bill Wilson.

_____ b. There is a twelve-step program available for just about every problem people face.

_____ c. Alcoholics Anonymous is a successful twelve-step program to help people recover from drinking problems.

Correct Answers, Part A _____

Correct Answers, Part B _____

Total Correct Answers _____

Any substance that is able to hold two materials together by its natural adhesion is an adhesive. Glue, mucilage, paste, cement, and epoxy are all forms of adhesive. Some adhesives occur in nature or are made easily from plant or animal materials. Others are made from synthetic materials. Adhesives can provide fastening in some cases in which mechanical fasteners, such as nails, staples, or clamps, might work poorly or not at all. Adhesives have a wide range of uses, from holding stamps on envelopes to holding heat-dissipating tiles to the exterior of a space shuttle.

Adhesives hold materials together by flowing into every nook and crevice of the materials' surfaces. The surfaces must be clean to allow the adhesive to "wet" each surface properly. Most adhesives are liquid or at least tacky. A few adhesives are powders or solids; they depend on heat and pressure to liquefy them. An adhesive creates a close bond between the surface molecules of the materials it holds together. The closer the two surfaces fit together, the stronger the bond. So a thin adhesive bond is stronger than a thick one.

One principal advantage of adhesives is that they easily bond particles, fibers, and films that would be difficult or impossible to bond by any other means. Examples are the abrasives on sandpaper and the glass, nylon, and polyester fibers in many automobile tires. Adhesives also bond the coatings on certain types of paper, such as those used in glossy magazines.

Another advantage of adhesives is that they distribute structural stresses more widely. This allows a stronger, lighter construction than is otherwise possible. For example, if a sheet of paper is tacked to a wall, pulling on the paper places stress only where the tacks go through it. The paper tears easily. If the sheet is glued to the wall, pulling on it places stress over the entire glued area. The paper is harder to remove. This factor comes into play in the making of aircraft and other industrial products.

There are other advantages. Most adhesives provide a barrier to moisture. Also, adhesives are often considerably faster and cheaper to use than mechanical fasteners.

Adhesives do have shortcomings. Adhesive bonds cannot be easily tested without weakening or destroying them. Nor can adhesive bonds be easily disassembled. Surfaces must be carefully prepared to ensure adhesion. Some adhesives require long periods of heat and pressure to set.

**Reading Time** _____

## Recalling Facts

1. Adhesives hold two materials together by
   - ❑ a. mechanical fasteners.
   - ❑ b. synthetic materials.
   - ❑ c. natural adhesion.

2. Most adhesives are
   - ❑ a. liquid.
   - ❑ b. solid.
   - ❑ c. slippery.

3. A thin adhesive bond is stronger than a thick one because
   - ❑ a. the two surfaces are closer together.
   - ❑ b. surface pressure is greater.
   - ❑ c. drying time is shortened.

4. A disadvantage of adhesives is that
   - ❑ a. adhesive bonds cannot be easily disassembled.
   - ❑ b. the bond is not very strong.
   - ❑ c. they are expensive.

5. Adhesives are used to bond glass, nylon, and polyester fibers in some
   - ❑ a. automobile tires.
   - ❑ b. sandpaper.
   - ❑ c. postage stamps.

## Understanding Ideas

6. Adhesives are a poor choice when
   - ❑ a. a moisture barrier is needed.
   - ❑ b. permanent bonding is required.
   - ❑ c. temporary bonding is required.

7. The most effective way to bond two surfaces of a paper airplane is by
   - ❑ a. stapling.
   - ❑ b. gluing.
   - ❑ c. nailing.

8. An adhesive would not be practical for
   - ❑ a. hanging a hook on a tile wall.
   - ❑ b. hanging a wreath on a door.
   - ❑ c. sealing an envelope.

9. A mechanical fastener might be preferable to an adhesive
   - ❑ a. to hang a picture on the wall.
   - ❑ b. to attach a photograph to a scrapbook page.
   - ❑ c. to hang a wallpaper border around a room.

10. An adhesive is likely to be less effective if
    - ❑ a. surfaces of the material to be bonded are not clean.
    - ❑ b. the materials to be bonded are metals.
    - ❑ c. the bonded materials are left outdoors in the rain.

## 15 | B | A Sticky Invention

Everyone uses self-sticking notes—those sticky little squares of colored paper—to leave messages and mark places in books. Their great advantage is that they can be peeled off easily without leaving a mark and can even be restuck someplace else.

The manufacturer of those notes almost missed out on a product that has taken its place in everyday life. The secret of self-sticking notes was discovered by accident in 1968 at a laboratory where research into super-glue was being conducted.

One batch of adhesive produced in the lab was so weak that the company, 3M (Minnesota Mining and Manufacturing Company), decided it was useless. A chemist named Art Fry found a use for the weak glue, however. A choir singer, he used the glue to make bookmarks for his hymn book. When the bookmarks were no longer needed, they could be removed without damaging the page.

Fry saw the marketing potential of this glue and tried to persuade the company that it was throwing away an idea that could have uses worldwide. After quite a while, he succeeded in convincing the company. In 1980, 3M began selling pads of notepaper with a strip of adhesive along one edge.

1. **Recognizing Words in Context**

   Find the word *conducted* in the passage. One definition below is a *synonym* for that word; it means the same or almost the same thing. One definition is an *antonym;* it has the opposite or nearly opposite meaning. The other has a completely different meaning. Label the definitions S for *synonym,* A for *antonym,* and D for *different.*

   _____ a. performed

   _____ b. avoided

   _____ c. guided

2. **Distinguishing Fact from Opinion**

   Two of the statements below present *facts,* which can be proved correct. The other statement is an *opinion,* which expresses someone's thoughts or beliefs. Label the statements F for *fact* and O for *opinion.*

   _____ a. The batch of weak glue was useless.

   _____ b. A chemist named Art Fry used the weak glue to make bookmarks.

   _____ c. The 3M company began marketing self-sticking notepads in 1980.

## 3. Keeping Events in Order

Label the statements below 1, 2, and 3 to show the order in which the events happened.

_____ a. Art Fry used the weak glue to make bookmarks.

_____ b. The laboratory produced a batch of weak glue.

_____ c. Everyone uses self-sticking notes for messages.

## 4. Making Correct Inferences

Two of the statements below are correct *inferences,* or reasonable guesses. They are based on information in the passage. The other statement is an incorrect, or faulty, inference. Label the statements C for *correct* inference and F for *faulty* inference.

_____ a. The glue used on self-sticking notes is not related to superglue.

_____ b. Art Fry found an imaginative use for weak glue.

_____ c. Companies sometimes fail to recognize the potential of a product.

## 5. Understanding Main Ideas

One of the statements below expresses the main idea of the passage. One statement is too general, or too broad. The other explains only part of the passage; it is too narrow. Label the statements M for *main idea,* B for *too broad,* and N for *too narrow.*

_____ a. Adhesives have a wide range of uses.

_____ b. Art Fry used weak glue to make bookmarks.

_____ c. The invention of useful self-sticking notes came about as the result of a laboratory accident.

Correct Answers, Part A _____

Correct Answers, Part B _____

Total Correct Answers _____

In the broadest sense, ammunition includes any device used to carry a destructive force. Bullets, artillery shells, bombs, torpedoes, grenades, and explosive mines are all forms of ammunition. Rockets and guided missiles are sometimes considered ammunition.

The earliest ammunition probably was thrown rocks. Prehistoric peoples used slings to hurl rocks at prey or enemies. At first, they used small, smooth stones as ammunition in their slings. Over time, the ammunition changed. The ancient Phoenicians loaded their slings with molded lead pellets for greater range and deadlier force. The catapult, a mechanical slingshot, used huge rocks and large arrows or javelins as ammunition.

Prehistoric peoples later developed the bow and arrow. The first arrows were thin wooden shafts with stone arrowheads. Later ones had metal arrowheads.

Most forms of ammunition require a means of propelling the projectile to its target. Before the invention of gunpowder, propulsion came from the muscle energy of one or more people. A bow stored muscle energy until the string was released to shoot an arrow. Catapults used the muscle energy of several people to propel rocks. Gunpowder is a propellant that explodes, releasing chemical energy.

Early cannons fired projectiles made of stone, lead, iron, or bronze. The largest cannons shot stone projectiles. Their barrels could not withstand the high internal pressure produced by firing heavy metal cannonballs. Through the years, other kinds of projectiles were developed for artillery. These included canister and grapeshot, which were cases of small metal balls that could be loaded into a cannon as a single unit. The balls scattered after being fired, with lethal effect on enemy troops.

Crude explosive shells were developed by the 16th century. The shells consisted of hollow cannonballs filled with gunpowder plus a slow-burning fuse. A shell was fired after its fuse had been lit. During the 19th century, cast lead balls were replaced by bullet-shaped projectiles that provided greater range and accuracy.

In early firearms, the gunpowder was ignited by fire. Gunsmiths later modified small arms and some cannons to use the sparks from flint or steel to ignite the powder. In the early 19th century, the development of primers in the form of percussion caps provided a more reliable method of igniting gunpowder. These caps were made of a chemical that exploded when struck by a gun hammer. The chemical was contained in capsules of metal, foil, or paper.

**Reading Time** _____

## Recalling Facts

1. Any device used to carry a destructive force is considered
   - ❏ a. propulsion.
   - ❏ b. ammunition.
   - ❏ c. a firearm.

2. An early device for propelling huge rocks and arrows or javelins was called a
   - ❏ a. sling.
   - ❏ b. bow.
   - ❏ c. catapult.

3. In early firearms, the gunpowder was ignited by
   - ❏ a. chemicals.
   - ❏ b. pressure.
   - ❏ c. fire.

4. The earliest means of propulsion came from
   - ❏ a. rocks.
   - ❏ b. guided missiles.
   - ❏ c. muscle energy.

5. Crude explosive shells were developed by
   - ❏ a. ancient Phoenicia.
   - ❏ b. the 16th century.
   - ❏ c. the 20th century.

## Understanding Ideas

6. You can conclude from the article that large devices for propelling ammunition were devised for
   - ❏ a. defense purposes.
   - ❏ b. killing prey.
   - ❏ c. sport.

7. The advantage of gunpowder over previous propellants is that it
   - ❏ a. is cheaper.
   - ❏ b. does more damage.
   - ❏ c. ignites more easily.

8. You can conclude from the article that devices such as slings and bows gave prehistoric people
   - ❏ a. increased muscle energy.
   - ❏ b. explosive power.
   - ❏ c. greater range and accuracy.

9. You can conclude from the article that the effectiveness of ammunition depends on
   - ❏ a. its size.
   - ❏ b. when it was devised.
   - ❏ c. how it is propelled.

10. Bullets and bombs differ from the earliest forms of ammunition in that they require
    - ❏ a. ignition.
    - ❏ b. muscle energy.
    - ❏ c. internal pressure.

## 16 B    Sure Shot

One of the most famous sharpshooters of the Old West was Annie Oakley. Annie's father died when she was five, and her family was desperately poor. By the time Annie was eight, she was using her father's gun to hunt squirrels and rabbits for food. By her early teens, she began supplying local restaurants with quail and pheasant, earning enough money to help her family financially.

After the Civil War, target shooting became popular entertainment. Annie entered a contest against a well-known sharpshooter, Frank Butler, and won. Later they married, and the two began touring together. He taught her to read and write and became her business manager.

Unquestionably, Annie Oakley was a phenomenal markswoman. She could shoot the flame out on a candle or a coin out of someone's fingers. She could stand on the back of a galloping horse and shoot glass balls thrown into the air, or turn a handspring, grab her gun, and hit a moving target. She always thrilled and amazed her audience. She became world famous.

In 1912, Oakley retired a rich woman, although she did give an occasional exhibition to prove that she could still shoot. She celebrated her sixty-second birthday by shooting one hundred clay pigeons in a row.

1. **Recognizing Words in Context**

   Find the word *phenomenal* in the passage. One definition below is a *synonym* for that word; it means the same or almost the same thing. One definition is an *antonym;* it has the opposite or nearly opposite meaning. The other has a completely different meaning. Label the definitions S for *synonym,* A for *antonym,* and D for *different.*

   _____ a. ordinary

   _____ b. exceptional

   _____ c. personal

2. **Distinguishing Fact from Opinion**

   Two of the statements below present *facts,* which can be proved correct. The other statement is an *opinion,* which expresses someone's thoughts or beliefs. Label the statements F for *fact* and O for *opinion.*

   _____ a. Annie Oakley used her father's gun to shoot squirrels.

   _____ b. Oakley could shoot a coin out of someone's fingers.

   _____ c. Oakley thrilled and amazed every audience.

3. **Keeping Events in Order**

Label the statements below 1, 2, and 3 to show the order in which the events happened.

_____ a. Annie defeated Frank Butler in a shooting contest.

_____ b. Annie toured the world, demonstrating her skills.

_____ c. Annie helped support her family with her shooting.

4. **Making Correct Inferences**

Two of the statements below are correct *inferences,* or reasonable guesses. They are based on information in the passage. The other statement is an incorrect, or faulty, inference. Label the statements C for *correct* inference and F for *faulty* inference.

_____ a. Annie Oakley had exceptional shooting skills.

_____ b. Annie's success was pure luck.

_____ c. Annie worked very hard at her chosen career.

5. **Understanding Main Ideas**

One of the statements below expresses the main idea of the passage. One statement is too general, or too broad. The other explains only part of the passage; it is too narrow. Label the statements M for *main idea,* B for *too broad,* and N for *too narrow.*

_____ a. Being an excellent shot can bring fame.

_____ b. Annie Oakley's shooting skills took her from poverty to fame and riches.

_____ c. Annie Oakley could shoot the flame out on a candle or a coin out of someone's fingers.

Correct Answers, Part A _____

Correct Answers, Part B _____

Total Correct Answers _____

The author of *Robinson Crusoe* was Daniel Defoe. A man of many talents, he was not only a writer, but also a business person, secret agent, and journalist.

Daniel Defoe was born in London, England, in about 1660. His father, James Foe, was a butcher. The Foes were Dissenters who did not believe in certain practices of the Church of England. Daniel was brought up in the strict, yet independent beliefs of the Dissenters.

At 14, Daniel was sent to a Dissenters' academy. In addition to traditional Latin and Greek, he studied French, Italian, Spanish, and history. He became especially well educated in geography. Although he studied for the ministry, Daniel went into business.

Engaged in foreign trade, Daniel visited France and lived in Spain for a time. Meanwhile, he was writing and speculating financially. He began to use the name Defoe, which may have been the original Flemish family name.

Defoe soon became more interested in writing than in conducting business. He was concerned about the many problems of the day. In pamphlets, verse, and periodicals, he called for reforms and advances in religious practices, economics, social welfare, and politics. In 1698, he wrote "Essay on Projects." In it, Defoe suggested a national bank, reformed bankruptcy laws, asylums, and academies of learning. He stressed the need for tolerance, often using satire for emphasis.

In 1702, Defoe wrote a pamphlet satirizing the persecution of Dissenters titled "The Shortest Way with the Dissenters." The government arrested him; for three days, he stood locked in irons while people brought him flowers. They admired his spirit. Defoe wrote of this experience.

After some months in prison, Defoe was released through the influence of Robert Harley, a politician who became his patron. Defoe then wrote political pamphlets for Harley and served as his secret agent working for the union of Scotland and England.

In 1704, Defoe started *The Review,* which was the first of many such periodicals with which he was connected. As people of that era did not care for fiction, Defoe wrote histories of pirates and thieves, spicing facts with imagination. In 1719, he published the novel *Robinson Crusoe,* which was drawn from the experiences of British sailor Alexander Selkirk. Like the character in the novel, Selkirk was marooned on a Pacific island for several years.

Defoe's other major works include *Moll Flanders* and *Roxana.* He died in London on April 24, 1731.

**Reading Time** _____

## Recalling Facts

1. Daniel Defoe was born in
   - ❏ a. Spain.
   - ❏ b. France.
   - ❏ c. England.

2. Dissenters were people who
   - ❏ a. disagreed with some practices of the Church of England.
   - ❏ b. agreed with the practices of the Church of England.
   - ❏ c. did not follow any organized religion.

3. Defoe went into business after studying to be a
   - ❏ a. lawyer.
   - ❏ b. teacher.
   - ❏ c. minister.

4. After writing a satire about the persecution of the Dissenters, Defoe
   - ❏ a. was imprisoned.
   - ❏ b. changed his name to Defoe.
   - ❏ c. moved to Scotland.

5. *Robinson Crusoe* was based on
   - ❏ a. Defoe's own travels.
   - ❏ b. the experiences of Alexander Selkirk, a British sailor.
   - ❏ c. Robert Harley's adventures.

## Understanding Ideas

6. Defoe's earliest works suggest that he might have made a good
   - ❏ a. doctor.
   - ❏ b. judge.
   - ❏ c. politician.

7. Defoe's use of satire exhibited his
   - ❏ a. serious nature.
   - ❏ b. acting ability.
   - ❏ c. sense of humor.

8. Defoe received flowers while in jail, which suggests that
   - ❏ a. he was wrongly imprisoned.
   - ❏ b. the government misestimated the popularity of his ideas.
   - ❏ c. all prisoners received flowers.

9. A good word to describe Daniel Defoe is
   - ❏ a. defiant.
   - ❏ b. timid.
   - ❏ c. indifferent.

10. Defoe would probably support the need for
    - ❏ a. greater understanding of differences among people and ideas.
    - ❏ b. state religions.
    - ❏ c. censorship of ideas.

## 17    B        Robinson Crusoe

Daniel Defoe based the novel *Robinson Crusoe* on an autobiography by a shipwreck victim named Alexander Selkirk. In Defoe's novel, Crusoe is shipwrecked and washes up on a rocky shore. At first grateful to be alive, he soon realizes that he is alone and without basic necessities like clothing, food, and weapons. Determined to survive, Crusoe salvages what he can from the wreck and builds a shelter.

Relying on his wits and what he can find on the island, Crusoe grows crops and captures wild goats for meat. He endures illness, storms, and many other hardships. Although desolated by loneliness, Crusoe does not give up. Years pass in this fashion. Then, on a trip to the other side of the island, Crusoe sees footprints—the first sign of human life in more than five years! Almost immediately, he realizes that the visitors to his island must be cannibals.

Crusoe strengthens his fort and lives in fear of capture. At one point, he is able to overcome his fear and rescues a young captive from the cannibals. He names the man Friday. Eventually, Crusoe and Friday are rescued, but not without more difficulties.

Today, people still read Defoe's novel, which was published in 1719. They enjoy its high adventure and its insights into the problems of loneliness and isolation.

### 1.  Recognizing Words in Context

Find the word *desolated* in the passage. One definition below is a *synonym* for that word; it means the same or almost the same thing. One definition is an *antonym;* it has the opposite or nearly opposite meaning. The other has a completely different meaning. Label the definitions S for *synonym*, A for *antonym,* and D for *different*.

_____ a. cheered

_____ b. miserable

_____ c. confused

### 2.  Distinguishing Fact from Opinion

Two of the statements below present *facts,* which can be proved correct. The other statement is an *opinion,* which expresses someone's thoughts or beliefs. Label the statements F for *fact* and O for *opinion.*

_____ a. Alexander Selkirk wrote an autobiography.

_____ b. Defoe's novel was published in 1719.

_____ c. People enjoy Defoe's novel today.

## 3. Keeping Events in Order

Label the statements below 1, 2, and 3 to show the order in which the events happened.

_____ a. Crusoe is shipwrecked.

_____ b. Crusoe sees footprints on his island.

_____ c. Crusoe rescues a young man and names him Friday.

## 4. Making Correct Inferences

Two of the statements below are correct *inferences,* or reasonable guesses. They are based on information in the passage. The other statement is an incorrect, or faulty, inference. Label the statements C for *correct* inference and F for *faulty* inference.

_____ a. *Robinson Crusoe* is basically a survival tale.

_____ b. *Robinson Crusoe* is a true story.

_____ c. *Robinson Crusoe* explores the theme of isolation.

## 5. Understanding Main Ideas

One of the statements below expresses the main idea of the passage. One statement is too general, or too broad. The other explains only part of the passage; it is too narrow. Label the statements M for *main idea,* B for *too broad,* and N for *too narrow.*

_____ a. Daniel Defoe's *Robinson Crusoe* tells how Crusoe survives both physical hardship and isolation on a deserted island.

_____ b. Relying on his wits and what he can find, Crusoe grows crops and captures wild goats for meat.

_____ c. Daniel Defoe wrote *Robinson Crusoe.*

Correct Answers, Part A _____

Correct Answers, Part B _____

Total Correct Answers _____

## 18 A The Diesel Engine

Of all internal-combustion engines, the diesel engine is the most efficient. It can extract the greatest amount of mechanical energy from a given amount of fuel. It achieves this high level of performance by compressing air to high pressures before injecting tiny droplets of fuel into the combustion chamber.

High temperatures are created when air is highly compressed in a diesel engine. The heat causes the fuel to burn without ignition by spark plugs. So unlike gasoline engines, diesel engines do not require spark plugs. Very large diesel engines, which are used for stationary power production and to power boats and ships, can be twice as efficient as a conventional gasoline engine. However, the high pressures created inside diesel engines make heavy engines with thick cylinder walls necessary. High weight and the need for careful maintenance of the fuel-injection system have made the diesel engine most useful for trucks, buses, ships, movable industrial-power systems, and diesel-electric railroad locomotives. Its weight makes the diesel engine unsuitable for use in aircraft, and it has found only limited acceptance in automobiles.

The heart of the diesel engine is its fuel-injection system. In the system, each cylinder has a separate fuel pump. This pump can develop pressures in excess of a thousand pounds per square inch (70 kilograms per square centimeter) to force a measured amount of oil through very small nozzle holes into the cylinder. The high pressures coupled with the small holes cause the atomization of the fuel. Various types of oils can be used for diesel engines. The most commonly used oil, called diesel fuel, is similar to the oil used in home heating systems.

In the widely used four-stroke engine, the piston draws air into the cylinder during the first stroke. During the second stroke, the air is compressed in the cylinder to about one-fifteenth of its original volume. At this point, a predetermined amount of finely atomized fuel, or fuel in the form of very small droplets, is injected into the cylinder through the fuel pump. The high air temperature in the cylinder causes the fuel to burn rapidly without the use of a spark plug. The high-temperature, combusted gas pushes the piston to the cylinder's bottom, delivering power to the crankshaft during the third stroke. During the fourth stroke, the low-pressure, combusted gases are pushed through the exhaust port. Thus, only one stroke of four delivers power.

**Reading Time** _____

## Recalling Facts

1. The diesel engine is
   - ❏ a. an external-combustion engine.
   - ❏ b. an internal-combustion engine.
   - ❏ c. a compression engine.

2. Unlike a gasoline engine, the diesel engine does not require
   - ❏ a. pistons.
   - ❏ b. spark plugs.
   - ❏ c. cylinders.

3. The diesel engine is unsuitable for aircraft because of its
   - ❏ a. cost.
   - ❏ b. weight.
   - ❏ c. oil requirements.

4. The diesel engine operates using
   - ❏ a. gasoline.
   - ❏ b. a fuel-injection system.
   - ❏ c. a heat pump.

5. In a diesel engine, power is delivered once every
   - ❏ a. two strokes.
   - ❏ b. three strokes.
   - ❏ c. four strokes.

## Understanding Ideas

6. The biggest advantage of the diesel engine is its
   - ❏ a. weight.
   - ❏ b. efficiency.
   - ❏ c. durability.

7. For its operation, the diesel engine depends on
   - ❏ a. water.
   - ❏ b. compressed air.
   - ❏ c. air conditioning.

8. If the walls of a diesel engine were thin, it is likely that the engine would
   - ❏ a. operate more efficiently.
   - ❏ b. burst from high internal pressure.
   - ❏ c. burst from high external pressure.

9. Diesel fuel is actually a type of
   - ❏ a. gasoline.
   - ❏ b. oil.
   - ❏ c. heating system.

10. You can conclude from the article that in order to function, all engines require
    - ❏ a. fuel combustion.
    - ❏ b. internal fuel combustion.
    - ❏ c. external fuel combustion.

# Rudolph Diesel

Born in 1858, Rudolph Diesel studied engineering in Germany and then worked for a Swiss machine manufacturer. He became interested in internal-combustion engines—engines that burn fuel internally instead of using power from an outside fuel chamber, as most engines did at the time. Diesel developed an engine that used coal dust as fuel. He received a German patent for it in 1892, but others had invented similar engines, and Diesel was not satisfied.

In 1893, Diesel published a paper on high-efficiency internal-combustion engines. His idea was to compress air in a chamber, thus making it very hot. Fuel sprayed directly into the chamber would ignite when it met the hot air.

Many of Diesel's fellow engineers scoffed at his theory; they thought it was impractical. However, Diesel managed to convince a manufacturing company to work on a practical engine that followed his principles, and the engine worked.

Diesel soon realized that coal dust was not a practical fuel. He switched to fuel oil mixed with air for ignition. The new engine was an immediate success, and soon diesel engines were in use worldwide. Today they drive buses, locomotives, trucks, ships, and factory machines all over the world.

1. **Recognizing Words in Context**

   Find the word *scoffed* in the passage. One definition below is a *synonym* for that word; it means the same or almost the same thing. One definition is an *antonym;* it has the opposite or nearly opposite meaning. The other has a completely different meaning. Label the definitions S for *synonym*, A for *antonym*, and D for *different*.

   _____ a. sneered

   _____ b. wondered

   _____ c. applauded

2. **Distinguishing Fact from Opinion**

   Two of the statements below present *facts*, which can be proved correct. The other statement is an *opinion*, which expresses someone's thoughts or beliefs. Label the statements F for *fact* and O for *opinion*.

   _____ a. Diesel's theory was impractical.

   _____ b. Diesel received a German patent for an engine he invented.

   _____ c. Rudolph Diesel studied engineering in Germany.

## 3. Keeping Events in Order

Label the statements below 1, 2, and 3 to show the order in which the events happened.

_____ a. Diesel went to work for a Swiss machine manufacturer.

_____ b. Diesel published a paper on internal-combustion engines.

_____ c. Diesel changed his fuel from coal dust to fuel oil.

## 4. Making Correct Inferences

Two of the statements below are correct *inferences,* or reasonable guesses. They are based on information in the passage. The other statement is an incorrect, or faulty, inference. Label the statements C for *correct* inference and F for *faulty* inference.

_____ a. Diesel did not give up easily.

_____ b. Diesel's ideas were not very original.

_____ c. Diesel focused his life's work on improving the internal-combustion engine.

## 5. Understanding Main Ideas

One of the statements below expresses the main idea of the passage. One statement is too general, or too broad. The other explains only part of the passage; it is too narrow. Label the statements M for *main idea,* B for *too broad,* and N for *too narrow.*

_____ a. When Diesel switched from coal dust to fuel oil, his engine was an immediate success.

_____ b. Rudolph Diesel and others invented internal-combustion engines.

_____ c. Rudolph Diesel spent his career developing the engine that bears his name.

Correct Answers, Part A _____

Correct Answers, Part B _____

Total Correct Answers _____

A limited selection of food that is prepared in advance and served within minutes of being ordered is known as fast food. Fast-food restaurants are popular eating places in the United States. For decades, hot dog, hamburger, and other snack stands have offered almost instant meals. These were usually owned and operated by different owners. Modern fast-food establishments, however, are usually not separately owned. Many of them are parts of large national or regional chains. This enables them to offer a great number, yet still limited selection, of dishes at nominal prices and still make an adequate profit.

Because they are chains, the food that fast-food restaurants sell is virtually the same at every outlet. They generally specialize in one kind of food such as hamburgers, pizza, chicken, or tacos. This specialization and standardization is maintained by the terms of a franchise agreement. The agreement requires every outlet to offer the same type of service and to buy its inventory from approved wholesalers. Some chains, however, have begun to diversify. One hamburger chain, for example, has experimented with pizza, fried chicken, and submarine sandwiches; and many restaurants now serve breakfast.

Apart from immediate service and standardized products, fast-food establishments differ from other restaurants by selling food over a counter. There may be tables so that food may be eaten on the premises, but customers are not seated and offered a menu. Some restaurant chains provide quick service and standardized menus but operate more like regular restaurants in that they provide table service and offer a wider range of food and beverages. Dining in these establishments is generally a leisurely, but more expensive experience than that offered by fast-food outlets.

Most fast-food meals are high in fat and sodium and low in fiber and nutrients. Chicken or fish entrees offer lower-fat alternatives. However, fried patties and nuggets may derive more than 50 percent of their calories from fat. This number is well over the 30 percent recommended by public-health organizations. Some chains provide reduced-fat hamburgers, salads, low-fat milk, and juices.

American-style fast-food emporiums now can be found around the globe. In the late 1980s, American fast-food companies began establishing outlets in communist nations. Pizza Hut opened a branch in the former Soviet Union in 1990, and by 1991 the McDonald's in Moscow's Red Square, serving 27,000 customers per day, had become more popular with tourists than Lenin's tomb.

**Reading Time** _____

## Recalling Facts

1. American fast-food franchises are noted for
   - ❏ a. standardized products.
   - ❏ b. fine dining.
   - ❏ c. diverse menus.

2. Fast-food establishments differ from other restaurants by
   - ❏ a. providing fast service.
   - ❏ b. selling food over a counter.
   - ❏ c. offering desserts.

3. Public-health organizations recommend that foods derive no more than
   - ❏ a. 10 percent of their calories from fat.
   - ❏ b. 50 percent of their calories from fat.
   - ❏ c. 30 percent of their calories from fat.

4. Most fast-food meals are
   - ❏ a. high in fat and sodium.
   - ❏ b. high in fat and low in sodium.
   - ❏ c. high in fiber and nutrients.

5. American fast-food companies are established
   - ❏ a. only in the United States.
   - ❏ b. mainly in Europe.
   - ❏ c. around the globe.

## Understanding Ideas

6. People who eat in fast-food restaurants have a desire to
   - ❏ a. eat healthy meals.
   - ❏ b. eat quickly.
   - ❏ c. enjoy a wide range of food.

7. You can conclude from the article that fast-food restaurants serve food that is
   - ❏ a. expensive.
   - ❏ b. low in price.
   - ❏ c. costly to produce.

8. You can conclude from the article that standardization and specialization help to
   - ❏ a. control food costs.
   - ❏ b. raise food prices.
   - ❏ c. enhance food quality.

9. The popularity of fast-food restaurants suggests that
   - ❏ a. people prefer fast-food restaurants to conventional restaurants.
   - ❏ b. fast-food restaurants meet the needs of busy, budget-minded people.
   - ❏ c. food that is prepared in advance is superior over food that is cooked to order.

10. American fast-food restaurants can be found around the globe, which suggests that
    - ❏ a. there is a market for American-style foods in foreign nations.
    - ❏ b. other nations do not have other kinds of restaurants.
    - ❏ c. people from other nations want to live in America.

## 19  B  Hamburger University

In 1961, McDonald's top managers saw a problem. They wanted to guarantee that food in all their restaurants would be uniform and served with the same speed and efficiency everywhere. Then McDonald's French fries would be the same from California to Maine. But different restaurants were getting widely different results, even though all were using basically the same business plans and ingredients.

Top management decided to bring managers together for a training program. The first training sessions were held in the basement of a nearby restaurant. But the McDonald's chain grew rapidly, and the demand for training got bigger, too. McDonald's purchased land near its headquarters in Illinois and built a training center, which management named Hamburger University. There, new managers learn how to encourage teamwork among employees, write business plans, and care for restaurant equipment. Advanced courses cover human relations and communications skills as well as the fine points of business management.

Today, McDonald's uses exciting new technology to train its people around the world. Management students from Moscow to China attend classes by means of satellite communication and video technology. The food there may be different, but the quality will be the same, thanks to Hamburger U.

1. **Recognizing Words in Context**

   Find the word *uniform* in the passage. One definition below is a *synonym* for that word; it means the same or almost the same thing. One definition is an *antonym;* it has the opposite or nearly opposite meaning. The other has a completely different meaning. Label the definitions S for *synonym,* A for *antonym,* and D for *different.*

   _____ a. edible

   _____ b. alike

   _____ c. different

2. **Distinguishing Fact from Opinion**

   Two of the statements below present *facts,* which can be proved correct. The other statement is an *opinion,* which expresses someone's thoughts or beliefs. Label the statements F for *fact* and O for *opinion.*

   _____ a. McDonald's held its first training sessions in a restaurant.

   _____ b. McDonald's named its training center Hamburger University.

   _____ c. McDonald's uses exciting new technology for training.

### 3. Keeping Events in Order

Label the statements below 1, 2, and 3 to show the order in which the events happened.

_____ a. McDonald's managers saw a need for training.

_____ b. Hamburger University was established.

_____ c. McDonald's began using satellite communication for training sessions.

### 4. Making Correct Inferences

Two of the statements below are correct *inferences,* or reasonable guesses. They are based on information in the passage. The other statement is an incorrect, or faulty, inference. Label the statements C for *correct* inference and F for *faulty* inference.

_____ a. Well-managed restaurants are important to McDonald's.

_____ b. McDonald's emphasizes training over food preparation.

_____ c. McDonald's uses up-to-date training methods.

### 5. Understanding Main Ideas

One of the statements below expresses the main idea of the passage. One statement is too general, or too broad. The other explains only part of the passage; it is too narrow. Label the statements M for *main idea,* B for *too broad,* and N for *too narrow.*

_____ a. Restaurants have training programs for managers.

_____ b. McDonald's purchased land near its headquarters in Illinois and built a training center, which the company named Hamburger University.

_____ c. A need for training led McDonald's to establish Hamburger University, a training center that trains its managers around the world.

Correct Answers, Part A _____

Correct Answers, Part B _____

Total Correct Answers _____

Fires are fought almost every day in most countries. Millions of fires start each year and cause great destruction of property and much human suffering. Fire can start almost anywhere at any time if conditions are suitable. All that is needed is the oxygen in air, fuel, and a spark, or some other source of ignition. Fire can involve flammable liquids, combustible gases, and solid materials. Fire may burn slowly, smoldering, or it may flash suddenly over a large area. Fire may cause some burning substances to explode with great force, making windows break and walls fall, or it may burn a building or a forest with such intensity that it cannot be extinguished until all the fuel is consumed.

Thus, fire fighting is a dangerous occupation, and it must be done carefully, safely, and efficiently. For example, firefighters must wear full protective clothing when fighting any fire. A firefighter who enters a burning building should wear a self-contained breathing apparatus. Smoke inhalation is the cause of the greatest number of firefighter injuries.

Fortunately, the great majority of fires are discovered while they are still small and easily controlled or put out. The three means of extinguishing fire are by cooling, smothering, or separating the fuel from the fire. Water from a sprinkler head or a hose nozzle is a means of cooling because it absorbs the heat of a fire. Covering an oil fire with a layer of foam is an example of smothering, or depriving the fire of oxygen. The raking or digging of a fire line in grass, brush, or a forest is an example of separating fuel from the heat.

Everyone should learn how to extinguish small fires safely and how to behave in more serious fires. All families should practice exit drills so that everyone knows what to do in a fire emergency.

The simplest extinguishing devices for a family to have at home are a garden hose and portable fire extinguishers. In warm weather, the hose can be kept attached to an outdoor faucet. In cold weather, it may be attached to a faucet indoors by an adapter. Water should not be used on kitchen stove fires or on electrical equipment, but it is useful for fires in wastebaskets, furniture, sawdust, and wood shavings and for exterior fires. Portable fire extinguishers should be used on fires involving grease, oil, and electrical equipment.

**Reading Time** _____

## Recalling Facts

1. All that is needed to start a fire is a source of ignition, fuel, and
   - ❏ a. smoke.
   - ❏ b. gases.
   - ❏ c. oxygen.

2. When fighting a fire, firefighters are required to
   - ❏ a. carry hoses.
   - ❏ b. breathe slowly.
   - ❏ c. wear full protective clothing.

3. The greatest number of firefighter injuries is caused by
   - ❏ a. burns.
   - ❏ b. fatigue.
   - ❏ c. smoke inhalation.

4. The three means of extinguishing fire are by removing the fuel, smothering, or
   - ❏ a. ventilating.
   - ❏ b. cooling.
   - ❏ c. stoking.

5. Water should not be used to extinguish
   - ❏ a. electrical fires.
   - ❏ b. wood fires.
   - ❏ c. paper fires.

## Understanding Ideas

6. You can conclude from the article that portable fire extinguishers
   - ❏ a. are difficult to operate.
   - ❏ b. are too heavy to lift.
   - ❏ c. do not contain water.

7. You can conclude from the article that knowing what to do in a fire emergency
   - ❏ a. can save lives.
   - ❏ b. requires years of training.
   - ❏ c. prevents fires.

8. A self-contained breathing apparatus prevents
   - ❏ a. fuel consumption.
   - ❏ b. shortage of breath.
   - ❏ c. smoke inhalation.

9. Fires that cannot be extinguished by smothering or cooling will burn
   - ❏ a. indefinitely.
   - ❏ b. until there is no more fuel.
   - ❏ c. until an explosion takes place.

10. The article suggests that many home fires
    - ❏ a. require firefighters.
    - ❏ b. can be put out quickly.
    - ❏ c. cause serious damage.

# Early Firefighters

Fires plagued colonial American homes, with their candlelight and open fireplaces. The cry of "Fire!" initiated a bucket brigade. People formed a line to the nearest water source, filled buckets, and handed them along. Unfortunately, though, once a house fire got started, the house usually burned to the ground. In 1717, twenty Boston citizens formed the first volunteer fire department. Their equipment was minimal; a firefighter carried two buckets, a sack for household goods, and a few tools to take apart furniture. No one expected to save a burning house.

In 1720, "water engines" were developed in England. These were tubs on wheels. They had pumps that could squirt water on a fire. The tub still had to be filled from buckets, but it was a significant improvement. Boston bought six of these water engines and organized its firefighters into districts. Each district had a fire warden, volunteers, and its own water engine.

Gradually, water engines, now called fire engines, were improved with hoses to get the water closer to the fire and pipes to carry water from the water source to the tub. In the 1830s, horses replaced people for pulling equipment, and steam engines took over the job of pumping. By 1900, all American cities had trained firefighters and fire horses to draw steam fire engines.

1. **Recognizing Words in Context**

   Find the word *initiated* in the passage. One definition below is a *synonym* for that word; it means the same or almost the same thing. One definition is an *antonym;* it has the opposite or nearly opposite meaning. The other has a completely different meaning. Label the definitions S for *synonym*, A for *antonym,* and D for *different*.

   _____ a. started

   _____ b. ended

   _____ c. required

2. **Distinguishing Fact from Opinion**

   Two of the statements below present *facts,* which can be proved correct. The other statement is an *opinion,* which expresses someone's thoughts or beliefs. Label the statements F for *fact* and O for *opinion.*

   _____ a. By 1900, all American cities had trained firefighters and fire horses.

   _____ b. Boston firefighters were courageous.

   _____ c. The English developed "water engines."

3. **Keeping Events in Order**

Label the statements below 1, 2, and 3 to show the order in which the events happened.

_____ a. Boston bought six "water engines."

_____ b. Boston citizens formed a volunteer fire department.

_____ c. Horses began pulling fire equipment.

4. **Making Correct Inferences**

Two of the statements below are correct *inferences,* or reasonable guesses. They are based on information in the passage. The other statement is an incorrect, or faulty, inference. Label the statements C for *correct* inference and F for *faulty* inference.

_____ a. Colonial Americans feared and dreaded fire.

_____ b. People worked continually to improve the way they fought fires.

_____ c. Volunteer fire departments in Boston were unorganized.

5. **Understanding Main Ideas**

One of the statements below expresses the main idea of the passage. One statement is too general, or too broad. The other explains only part of the passage; it is too narrow. Label the statements M for *main idea,* B for *too broad,* and N for *too narrow.*

_____ a. From colonial times to 1900, fire fighting developed from bucket brigades to organized volunteers and then to trained fire departments.

_____ b. Fire fighting has changed since colonial times.

_____ c. By 1900, all American cities had trained fire-fighters and fire horses to draw steam fire engines.

Correct Answers, Part A _____

Correct Answers, Part B _____

Total Correct Answers _____

Properly set off by trained people, fireworks are safe and make a beautiful display against the evening sky. However, the use of fireworks by untrained people often leads to injury and to property damage. For this reason, the general use of fireworks is often against the law.

The scientific name for fireworks is *pyrotechnics,* from Greek words meaning "fire arts." The propelling and exploding force in fireworks comes from a combination of saltpeter, sulfur, and charcoal. The same substances make up gunpowder. Historians believe that fireworks were invented before gunpowder. They think gunpowder was developed as a result of experimenting with different quantities of the substances in the mixture. Thus, fireworks existed before guns, and the first firearms hurled flaming materials.

Fireworks were manufactured in Italy as early as 1540. By the 1600s, they were widely used in England and France. Most of the varieties known today, such as display rockets, aerial bombs, pinwheels, and fountains, were used in this early period. For centuries, the Chinese set off fireworks to celebrate their holidays. However, it was not until the middle of the 19th century that the United States adopted the custom of shooting off fireworks to celebrate Independence Day.

Fireworks serve as the basis of many useful products. Railroad trains, trucks, and cross-country buses carry red flares, which are placed behind stalled vehicles to avert collisions. Airplanes carry parachute flares to light up the ground area for forced landings at night. Rockets, Roman candles, and blue Bengal lights were long used as signals between vessels at sea and from ship to shore, and rockets still are used as signals of distress. In World War I, advancing infantry detachments sent information to the artillery in the rear by rocket signals. In World War II, rockets projected from airplanes, ground vehicles, and ships were used by the armies on both sides.

Unfortunately, the careless handling of fireworks causes many injuries every year. Sometimes these injuries lead to death. Property damage in the United States caused by the mishandling of fireworks may exceed more than 1.5 million dollars every year. Losses due to fireworks have been reduced through organizations interested in fire prevention and human welfare. Such groups urge the adoption of laws that forbid or limit the sale of fireworks to retail purchasers. These laws usually permit the display of fireworks under proper supervision for special events and civic celebrations.

**Reading Time** _____

## Recalling Facts

1. The scientific name for fireworks is
   - ❏ a. parachute flares.
   - ❏ b. Roman candles.
   - ❏ c. pyrotechnics.

2. Fireworks came into existence
   - ❏ a. before gunpowder.
   - ❏ b. along with gunpowder.
   - ❏ c. after gunpowder.

3. Rockets set off at sea
   - ❏ a. celebrate Chinese holidays.
   - ❏ b. signal distress.
   - ❏ c. signal time.

4. Property damage from fireworks
   - ❏ a. exceeds 1 million dollars annually.
   - ❏ b. is minimal.
   - ❏ c. increases every year.

5. The United States did not begin using fireworks to help celebrate Independence Day until
   - ❏ a. the early 1600s.
   - ❏ b. the mid-1900s.
   - ❏ c. World War II.

## Understanding Ideas

6. You can conclude from the article that fireworks are
   - ❏ a. used primarily for entertainment.
   - ❏ b. no longer useful.
   - ❏ c. both entertaining and useful.

7. You can conclude from the article that fireworks used as signals are
   - ❏ a. not effective.
   - ❏ b. more effective at night.
   - ❏ c. more effective during the day.

8. The article suggests that fireworks should be
   - ❏ a. outlawed.
   - ❏ b. set off only by trained people.
   - ❏ c. available to everyone.

9. From the article, you can conclude that groups working to change laws regarding fireworks in the United States
   - ❏ a. want to protect people.
   - ❏ b. dislike fireworks.
   - ❏ c. want to ban fireworks entirely.

10. It is likely that damage done to property from fireworks is a result of
    - ❏ a. fires from explosions.
    - ❏ b. poor planning.
    - ❏ c. excessive noise.

Fireworks originated in China, where people known as alchemists experimented with chemicals for their religious rituals. Around 850, they came up with explosive powder, which they used mostly for its noise and flashes of light.

When the explosive powder reached Europe around 1400, it inspired the military cannon, but it was also used for fireworks. Skyrockets became a popular way to celebrate. In America, Captain John Smith fired off a few in Jamestown in 1608 to impress the native people.

During the eighteenth century, fireworks were developed into the standard forms familiar to viewers today, but colors were limited to white and orange. Then in the 1830s, makers began adding metal salts that give off color when they are burned. By 1900, newly discovered metals, especially aluminum, added brilliance as well.

Through the nineteenth century, most fireworks displays reenacted battles—the flash and crash of bombs bursting in air. Some fireworks makers developed set pieces—frameworks lighted to create pictures in fire. In this century, fireworks shows have become more elaborate and awe-inspiring. Today's fireworks concentrate on rapid displays high in the air, splashing brilliant colors across the night sky. Fireworks are eternally popular, but professionals warn that they are dangerous. Most states have stringent laws governing their sale and use.

1. **Recognizing Words in Context**

Find the word *stringent* in the passage. One definition below is a *synonym* for that word; it means the same or almost the same thing. One definition is an *antonym*; it has the opposite or nearly opposite meaning. The other has a completely different meaning. Label the definitions S for *synonym*, A for *antonym*, and D for *different*.

_____ a. written

_____ b. strict

_____ c. relaxed

2. **Distinguishing Fact from Opinion**

Two of the statements below present *facts*, which can be proved correct. The other statement is an *opinion*, which expresses someone's thoughts or beliefs. Label the statements F for *fact* and O for *opinion*.

_____ a. The Chinese invented explosive powder.

_____ b. Metal salts added color to fireworks.

_____ c. Today's fireworks shows are awe-inspiring.

### 3. Keeping Events in Order

Label the statements below 1, 2, and 3 to show the order in which the events happened.

_____ a. Explosive powder reached Europe and inspired the military cannon.

_____ b. Fireworks makers added color to fireworks.

_____ c. The Chinese used fireworks in religious rituals.

### 4. Making Correct Inferences

Two of the statements below are correct *inferences,* or reasonable guesses. They are based on information in the passage. The other statement is an incorrect, or faulty, inference. Label the statements C for *correct* inference and F for *faulty* inference.

_____ a. Fireworks have always fascinated people.

_____ b. Fireworks shows are expensive to produce.

_____ c. Laws governing fireworks are necessary for safety.

### 5. Understanding Main Ideas

One of the statements below expresses the main idea of the passage. One statement is too general, or too broad. The other explains only part of the passage; it is too narrow. Label the statements M for *main idea,* B for *too broad,* and N for *too narrow.*

_____ a. Fireworks developed over several centuries.

_____ b. Today's fireworks concentrate on rapid displays high in the air, splashing brilliant colors across the night sky.

_____ c. Fireworks, developed from gunpowder between the sixteenth and the eighteenth centuries, still awe and fascinate people.

Correct Answers, Part A _____

Correct Answers, Part B _____

Total Correct Answers _____

# The One That Got Away

Catching fish from oceans, lakes, and streams is not only the most popular but probably the oldest pastime pursued by human beings. Thousands of years ago people caught fish in nets and traps woven out of vines. They also fashioned hooks from bone, stone, and thorns and baited them with worms, grubs, and insects. The term *fishing* applies to the act of catching a fish from its natural home, the water. Taking fish with nets and seines for food is called commercial fishing. Fishing with hook and line for fun is called sport fishing.

Perhaps the greatest appeal in fishing for fun is the opportunities it offers to get outdoors, to enjoy the companionship of friends, and to use new and varied skills to outwit the fish. In the United States, many state, federal, and private organizations spend millions of dollars annually to keep a plentiful supply of fish available for anglers to catch.

In fishing, a set of ethics exists based on consideration for others. One rule is to take no more fish than one needs. Some of the best anglers catch fish for the sport of it and then release them unharmed for someone else to catch. The sporting methods a person uses in catching fish and the consideration shown for others while fishing are the marks distinguishing a true fisher.

A wide range of equipment is readily available. The type of fishing gear needed depends on the kind of fish being sought, and there is gear available to fit almost any budget.

Still fishing is a technique of catching fish without moving from one spot—an anchored boat, a bridge, a dock, or a bank. It is perhaps the most common and least costly method. Because the fisher waits for the fish to come to the bait, patience is required. It is also one of the most delightful and relaxing methods of fishing because it offers the fisher an opportunity to enjoy the surrounding outdoor scene, visit with a companion, or nap in the shade of a tree along the bank and still be fishing.

Fishing is popular because anyone can fish, regardless of age, sex, or income. Fishing can be enjoyed from childhood to old age, individually or in groups, with little more investment than a cane pole and a few hooks. Within an hour from most homes, there is usually a place to fish.

**Reading Time** _____

## Recalling Facts

1. Catching fish with nets for food is called
   - ❑ a. sport fishing.
   - ❑ b. netting.
   - ❑ c. commercial fishing.

2. Another word for *net* is
   - ❑ a. *web*.
   - ❑ b. *seine*.
   - ❑ c. *trap*.

3. An ethical fisher
   - ❑ a. takes only as many fish as are needed.
   - ❑ b. always throws back unharmed fish.
   - ❑ c. uses only worms for bait.

4. Fishing with a hook and line for fun is called
   - ❑ a. still fishing.
   - ❑ b. sport fishing.
   - ❑ c. boat fishing.

5. To keep waters stocked with fish, government and private organizations
   - ❑ a. keep local waters free from pollution.
   - ❑ b. prohibit fishing in the waters.
   - ❑ c. spend millions of dollars annually.

## Understanding Ideas

6. Still fishing from a boat is probably not a sport for
   - ❑ a. patient people.
   - ❑ b. restless people.
   - ❑ c. older people.

7. Commercial fishers
   - ❑ a. use nets to catch more fish at one time.
   - ❑ b. fish for the sport of it.
   - ❑ c. practice catch and release methods.

8. You can conclude from the article that people who fish for sport
   - ❑ a. enjoy being outdoors.
   - ❑ b. have little else to do.
   - ❑ c. compete with the commercial fishers.

9. The major aim of a sport fisher is to
   - ❑ a. catch fish for food.
   - ❑ b. make money at fishing.
   - ❑ c. catch fish for fun.

10. You can conclude from the article that fishing is popular because it is
    - ❑ a. competitive.
    - ❑ b. relaxing and fun.
    - ❑ c. an ancient pastime.

In northern winters, when the temperature hovers around zero and lake surfaces are frozen two to three feet (0.6 to 0.9 of a meter) thick, avid sportspeople go ice fishing. The eager fishers may drive far out onto the frozen lakes to their favorite fishing spots, towing their fish houses. These are sheds, some tiny, some as big as a room, with a hole or holes cut through the floor.

Once a shed is in place, the fisher drills down through the ice, using a power auger, a corkscrew-like tool with a small engine, that can cut through three feet (0.9 of a meter) of ice in a few minutes. Then all the fisher has to do is bait a line and drop it through the hole. It's fishing with all the comforts of home, because many fish houses boast stoves, bunks, carpets, and comfortable chairs. They don't have refrigerators, though; the catch can be quick-frozen just by tossing it out the door.

Ice fishers usually leave their sheds in place throughout the winter fishing season. When spring warm-up begins, they tow the sheds back to solid ground and store them until next winter, when the fishing will be really fun again.

## 1. Recognizing Words in Context

Find the word *avid* in the passage. One definition below is a *synonym* for that word; it means the same or almost the same thing. One definition is an *antonym;* it has the opposite or nearly opposite meaning. The other has a completely different meaning. Label the definitions S for *synonym,* A for *antonym,* and D for *different.*

_____ a. bored

_____ b. needy

_____ c. eager

## 2. Distinguishing Fact from Opinion

Two of the statements below present *facts,* which can be proved correct. The other statement is an *opinion,* which expresses someone's thoughts or beliefs. Label the statements F for *fact* and O for *opinion.*

_____ a. Ice fishing is really fun.

_____ b. Fish houses are sheds with holes in the floor.

_____ c. A power auger can cut through three feet (0.9 of a meter) of ice in a few minutes.

### 3. Keeping Events in Order

Label the statements below 1, 2, and 3 to show the order in which the events happened.

_____ a. The ice freezes to a depth of two to three feet (0.6 to 0.9 meter).

_____ b. Fishers cut a hole in the ice with a power auger.

_____ c. People tow their fish houses onto the lake.

### 4. Making Correct Inferences

Two of the statements below are correct *inferences,* or reasonable guesses. They are based on information in the passage. The other statement is an incorrect, or faulty, inference. Label the statements C for *correct* inference and F for *faulty* inference.

_____ a. Ice fishing is only for people who can tolerate great cold.

_____ b. In some parts of the country, ice fishing is a popular sport.

_____ c. Ice fishing requires special equipment.

### 5. Understanding Main Ideas

One of the statements below expresses the main idea of the passage. One statement is too general, or too broad. The other explains only part of the passage; it is too narrow. Label the statements M for *main idea,* B for *too broad,* and N for *too narrow.*

_____ a. Ice fishing is a winter sport.

_____ b. A popular winter sport in the north is ice fishing from fish houses on the ice of frozen lakes.

_____ c. Some fish houses are equipped with stoves, bunks, and even comfortable chairs.

Correct Answers, Part A _____

Correct Answers, Part B _____

Total Correct Answers _____

Folk art is the product of a people, or folk; it is not the work of professional artists. Folk art is also not primitive art, which is art produced by preliterate, preurban societies. It is helpful to have a clear definition of what folk art is in order to identify, understand, and appreciate the many types of folk art.

Folk art is art that comes from groups of people who live within the general framework of a developed society. These folk artists are, for reasons of geographical or cultural isolation, largely cut off from the more advanced artistic productions of their time. Folk art is the art of peasants, shepherds, sailors, fisherfolk, artisans, and small tradespeople who live away from cultural centers in nations that are not heavily industrialized.

Folk art, then, consists of products of distinctive style made according to local tastes and to suit local needs. Objects of furniture, tools, toys, clothing, housing, musical instruments, weapons, religious figurines, and household utensils are some of the works to which the term *folk art* may be applied.

The folk artist, according to the standards of fine art, may be considered an amateur because of the lack of professional training in the fine arts. Art is not his or her primary occupation. The folk artist earns a living by other means and creates art for pleasure or for the enjoyment of others. Often lacking money, folk artists find it necessary to use inexpensive materials. The sculpture of a folk artist is not in marble or bronze, nor are his or her paintings in oils on canvas. Humbler sculptures are in wood, clay, iron, straw, and even ice or sugar. Paintings are on wood, cloth, or paper.

The fact that folk art thrives best in general isolation from the society in which it is created gives it honesty and authenticity. It is not beholden to outside influences, nor is it imitative of trends and schools of art. The rural atmosphere in which the folk artist lives forces improvisation: What is done is whatever seems interesting or imaginative.

Peasant societies tend to be conservative and to hold onto old ways of thinking and doing. They thus become repositories for many traditions, even discarded ones, in their art. Folk art reflects conventional, proverbial wisdom; old superstitions; sentimental themes; and religious beliefs that have long since ceased to be orthodox in the larger society.

**Reading Time** _____

## Recalling Facts

1. Folk art is made according to
   - ❏ a. artistic rules.
   - ❏ b. local tastes and needs.
   - ❏ c. economic needs.

2. Folk art survives best in
   - ❏ a. big cities.
   - ❏ b. a rural atmosphere.
   - ❏ c. museums.

3. Folk artists are considered
   - ❏ a. the only true artists.
   - ❏ b. professionals.
   - ❏ c. amateurs.

4. Folk artists are more likely to work with
   - ❏ a. oil paints and canvas.
   - ❏ b. marble and bronze.
   - ❏ c. wood and clay.

5. The effect of outside influences on folk art is
   - ❏ a. minimal.
   - ❏ b. substantial.
   - ❏ c. unavoidable.

## Understanding Ideas

6. Folk artists are inspired by
   - ❏ a. moral codes.
   - ❏ b. their imaginations.
   - ❏ c. popular art.

7. Folk art is likely to reflect
   - ❏ a. current world problems.
   - ❏ b. political beliefs.
   - ❏ c. local traditions.

8. As general society continues to expand, folk art is likely to
   - ❏ a. thrive.
   - ❏ b. become less popular.
   - ❏ c. become less unusual.

9. The term *folk art* frequently applies to items that are
   - ❏ a. practical.
   - ❏ b. primitive.
   - ❏ c. refined.

10. The main difference between folk art and other kinds of art is that folk art
    - ❏ a. is not influenced by current trends.
    - ❏ b. is created to give pleasure.
    - ❏ c. results from artistic imagination.

In parts of the European countryside, people have traditionally passed the long, cold winter evenings by carving wooden birds. Simple, yet elegant, the birds are carved from two pieces of pine about six inches long (about 15 centimeters) and about an inch square (6.45 square centimeters). The carver first soaks the wood in water for maximum pliability. The first piece becomes the bird's head, body, and tail. After shaping the head and body, the carver carves the tail in the shape of one feather and then slices it into thin layers. These the carver fans out into the graceful tail.

The second piece of wood becomes the wings. Like the tail, each wing is carved in the shape of one feather and then sliced and gently separated into a fan shape. Finally, the delicate wings are attached to the body with glue or a nail. The wood is left unpainted, so the birds are always white like doves—symbols of peace.

People hang the birds by strings from the ceiling, where they move with the air currents, seeming to fly. According to folk belief, the lovely white birds bring well-being to the household and are a sign of welcome and hospitality.

1. **Recognizing Words in Context**

Find the word *pliability* in the passage. One definition below is a *synonym* for that word; it means the same or almost the same thing. One definition is an *antonym*; it has the opposite or nearly opposite meaning. The other has a completely different meaning. Label the definitions S for *synonym*, A for *antonym*, and D for *different*.

_____ a. hardness

_____ b. softness

_____ c. wetness

2. **Distinguishing Fact from Opinion**

Two of the statements below present *facts*, which can be proved correct. The other statement is an *opinion*, which expresses someone's thoughts or beliefs. Label the statements F for *fact* and O for *opinion*.

_____ a. The birds are carved from pine.

_____ b. The birds are simple, yet elegant.

_____ c. The wings are attached to the body with glue or a nail.

## 3. Keeping Events in Order

Label the statements below 1, 2, and 3 to show the order in which the events happened.

_____ a. The carver soaks the wood in water.

_____ b. The wings are attached to the body.

_____ c. The carver carves the tail and then slices it into separate feathers.

## 4. Making Correct Inferences

Two of the statements below are correct *inferences*, or reasonable guesses. They are based on information in the passage. The other statement is an incorrect, or faulty, inference. Label the statements C for *correct* inference and F for *faulty* inference.

_____ a. Carved birds have traditional and symbolic meaning for the people who carve them.

_____ b. The white birds are folk art.

_____ c. Making a bird requires no particular skill.

## 5. Understanding Main Ideas

One of the statements below expresses the main idea of the passage. One statement is too general, or too broad. The other explains only part of the passage; it is too narrow. Label the statements M for *main idea*, B for *too broad*, and N for *too narrow*.

_____ a. Simple, yet elegant, the birds are carved from two pieces of pine.

_____ b. Some Europeans carve white birds.

_____ c. The carving of birds, part of European folk culture, creates objects of beauty and welcome.

Correct Answers, Part A _____

Correct Answers, Part B _____

Total Correct Answers _____

The destructive effects of explosives are much more spectacular than their peaceful uses. This is likely to make people forget that explosives are necessary for many of humans' most constructive efforts.

There are three basic types of explosives: mechanical, nuclear, and chemical. A mechanical explosive depends on a physical reaction such as overloading a container with compressed air. Such a device has some application in mining, in which the release of gas from chemical explosives may be undesirable. A nuclear explosive is one in which a sustained nuclear reaction can be made to take place with almost instant rapidity, releasing large amounts of energy. Chemical explosives account for virtually all explosive applications in engineering.

Explosives are of immense value in mining, quarrying, and engineering. They blast rocks and ores loose in mines and quarries; they also move great masses of earth and break coal into small pieces. Explosives are necessary for making fireworks, signal lights, and rockets. Farmers find explosives useful for breaking up boulders, blowing out stumps, felling trees, and loosening soil.

Explosives are also used in manufacturing aircraft. Blind rivets are needed when space limitations make conventional rivets impractical. An explosive rivet has a hollow space in the shank containing a small charge of heat-sensitive chemicals. When heat is applied to the head, an explosion takes place and expands the rivet shank tightly into the hole. The shank is sealed to eliminate noise and the ejection of metal fragments. Most explosive rivets are aluminum.

Explosives are sometimes used to bond various metals to each other. For example, when silver was removed from United States coinage, much of the so-called sandwich metal that replaced it was obtained by the explosive bonding of large slabs of metals, which, when bonded, were then rolled down to the required thickness. To achieve bonding, slabs of metals are placed parallel to each other and slightly apart. Then an explosive developed especially for the purpose is placed on the top slab; its detonation slams the slabs together with such force that they become welded. Stainless steel is often joined to ordinary steel in this manner. A valuable feature of explosion cladding is that it can frequently be applied to incompatible metals such as aluminum and steel or titanium and steel.

Finally, the very fine industrial-type diamonds used for grinding and polishing are produced by the carefully controlled action of explosives on carbon.

**Reading Time** _____

## Recalling Facts

1. The three basic types of explosives are mechanical, nuclear, and
   - ❏ a. atomic.
   - ❏ b. dynamic.
   - ❏ c. chemical.

2. A mechanical explosive depends on
   - ❏ a. a sustained explosion.
   - ❏ b. a physical reaction.
   - ❏ c. heat-sensitive chemicals.

3. Most explosive rivets are made of
   - ❏ a. stainless steel.
   - ❏ b. cast iron.
   - ❏ c. aluminum.

4. Sandwich metal is metal that has been
   - ❏ a. joined by explosive bonding.
   - ❏ b. bonded by glue.
   - ❏ c. rolled into layers.

5. Industrial-type diamonds are produced by the action of explosives on
   - ❏ a. steel.
   - ❏ b. carbon.
   - ❏ c. titanium.

## Understanding Ideas

6. The purpose of the article is to
   - ❏ a. educate readers about the constructive uses of explosives.
   - ❏ b. persuade readers that explosives should be banned from industrial uses.
   - ❏ c. educate readers about the dangers of explosives in the workplace.

7. Using explosives to mine stone in quarries is an example of explosives used
   - ❏ a. constructively.
   - ❏ b. destructively.
   - ❏ c. carelessly.

8. You can conclude from the article that explosives are
   - ❏ a. mostly destructive.
   - ❏ b. as useful as they are dangerous.
   - ❏ c. useful mainly for engineering purposes.

9. It is likely that silver was removed from United States coinage
   - ❏ a. to test bonding methods.
   - ❏ b. for economic reasons.
   - ❏ c. to increase costs.

10. Chemical explosives are not used for mining because
    - ❏ a. released gas would be harmful to humans.
    - ❏ b. the noise of the explosion would be too loud.
    - ❏ c. a nuclear reaction might take place.

## 24  B    The Man Who Invented Dynamite

Alfred Nobel was born in Sweden in 1833. His father had a factory in Russia that manufactured torpedoes and mines. Young Alfred grew up there, educated by a series of tutors. Later, he traveled to France and the United States before returning to Russia in 1852 to work for his father.

Nobel's experience with explosives led him to imagine their benevolent rather than destructive uses. He began to experiment with nitroglycerine, an explosive oil, trying to create a new explosive. He set up a small factory in Sweden to manufacture nitroglycerine. Unfortunately, the plant blew up, killing Nobel's younger brother. But Nobel persisted, and in 1867 he produced and patented a nitroglycerine explosive that was relatively safe. He named it "dynamite." Builders, miners, and farmers around the world soon began to use dynamite to make their work easier, as Nobel had hoped.

Nobel continued to experiment with explosives. His inventions made him a fortune. At his death, his money went to set up a foundation in his name. It awards prizes to the people who make the greatest contributions to humankind in the areas of physics, chemistry, economics, physiology or medicine, literature, and peace. Nobel prizes, awarded each year, greatly honor those who receive them.

1. **Recognizing Words in Context**

   Find the word *benevolent* in the passage. One definition below is a *synonym* for that word; it means the same or almost the same thing. One definition is an *antonym;* it has the opposite or nearly opposite meaning. The other has a completely different meaning. Label the definitions S for *synonym,* A for *antonym,* and D for *different.*

   _____ a. recreational

   _____ b. helpful

   _____ c. harmful

2. **Distinguishing Fact from Opinion**

   Two of the statements below present *facts,* which can be proved correct. The other statement is an *opinion,* which expresses someone's thoughts or beliefs. Label the statements F for *fact* and O for *opinion.*

   _____ a. Nobel was educated by tutors.

   _____ b. Nobel should be honored for his creation of dynamite.

   _____ c. Nobel produced dynamite in 1867.

## 3. Keeping Events in Order

Label the statements below 1, 2, and 3 to show the order in which the events happened.

_____ a. Nobel began experimenting with nitroglycerine.

_____ b. Nobel invented dynamite.

_____ c. Nobel's plant blew up.

## 4. Making Correct Inferences

Two of the statements below are correct *inferences,* or reasonable guesses. They are based on information in the passage. The other statement is an incorrect, or faulty, inference. Label the statements C for *correct* inference and F for *faulty* inference.

_____ a. Nobel's life shows that he valued humankind.

_____ b. Explosives have few peaceful uses.

_____ c. Nobel was a gifted inventor.

## 5. Understanding Main Ideas

One of the statements below expresses the main idea of the passage. One statement is too general, or too broad. The other explains only part of the passage; it is too narrow. Label the statements M for *main idea,* B for *too broad,* and N for *too narrow.*

_____ a. Alfred Nobel invented dynamite.

_____ b. Prizes named for famous people are awarded each year in many different fields.

_____ c. Alfred Nobel, the inventor of dynamite, set up the Nobel Prizes, which honor great achievements.

Correct Answers, Part A _____

Correct Answers, Part B _____

Total Correct Answers _____

# The First Dancers

It is the wedding of movement to music. It spans culture from soaring ballet leaps to the simple swaying at a high school prom. It is dance, a means of recreation and communication. It is perhaps the oldest, yet the most incompletely preserved, of the arts. Its origins are lost in prehistoric times, but, from the study of the most primitive peoples, it is known that men and women have always danced.

There are many kinds of dance. It can be a popular craze, like break dancing, or ballets that feature superstar performers. It can be folk dances that have been handed down through generations, such as the square dance, or ethnic dances that are primarily associated with a particular country. It can be modern dance or musical comedy dancing, both fields that were pioneered by American men and women.

Two sorts of dance evolved as cultures developed. Social dances celebrated births, commemorated deaths, and marked special events in between. Magical or religious dances asked the gods to end a famine, to provide rain, or to cure the sick. The medicine men of primitive cultures, whose powers to invoke the assistance of a god were feared and respected, are considered by many to be the first choreographers, or arrangers of formal dances.

Originally, rhythmic sound accompaniment was provided by the dancers themselves. Eventually, a separate rhythmic accompaniment evolved, probably played on animal skins stretched over wooden frames and made into drums or similar instruments. Later, melodies were added. These might have imitated birdcalls and other sounds of nature, or they might have been a vocal expression of the dancers' or musicians' state of mind. The rhythmic beat, however, was the most important element. This pulsation let all the dancers keep time together, and it helped them remember their movements, too.

Primitive dancers also shared certain gestures and movements that were drawn from their everyday lives. Farmers planting seeds swung their arms with unvarying regularity. People who were hungry rubbed a hand on their empty bellies. People who wanted to show respect or admiration bent down or bowed before another individual. These gestures, and others like them, were part of the earliest dances.

Other gestures originated as a means of expressing emotion. Caresses are universally taken to signify tender feelings. Clenched fists mean anger. Hopping up and down indicates excitement. Primitive dancers used all of these movements in their dances.

**Reading Time** _____

## Recalling Facts

1. Dances that have been handed down through generations are considered
   - ❏ a. folk dances.
   - ❏ b. ballets.
   - ❏ c. modern dance.

2. Two sorts of dances that evolved as cultures developed are social and
   - ❏ a. instrumental.
   - ❏ b. religious.
   - ❏ c. historical.

3. Arrangers of formal dances are called
   - ❏ a. musicians.
   - ❏ b. performers.
   - ❏ c. choreographers.

4. The first dance arrangers were probably
   - ❏ a. folk dancers.
   - ❏ b. medicine men.
   - ❏ c. farmers.

5. The most important element in sound that accompanied early dancing was
   - ❏ a. noise level.
   - ❏ b. rhythmic beat.
   - ❏ c. melody.

## Understanding Ideas

6. Formal dancing can best be described as
   - ❏ a. gestures expressing emotion.
   - ❏ b. rhythmic movement to music.
   - ❏ c. movement accompanied by sound.

7. A dance to celebrate a youth becoming an adult member of a community would be considered
   - ❏ a. a social dance.
   - ❏ b. a religious dance.
   - ❏ c. a ballet.

8. You can conclude from the article that early dancing
   - ❏ a. expressed no emotion.
   - ❏ b. was very emotional.
   - ❏ c. lacked energy.

9. Today's dancing is characterized by great
   - ❏ a. variety.
   - ❏ b. universal themes.
   - ❏ c. influences from the past.

10. The primary purpose of this article is
    - ❏ a. to persuade the reader.
    - ❏ b. to entertain the reader.
    - ❏ c. to educate the reader.

## 25　B　Our American Dance

Tap dancing probably has its roots in Africa. Most African cultures included tribal dances accompanied by drums as an important part of community life. The dances consisted of rhythmic foot-stomping and fluid hip movements. Enslaved people brought to this country continued to drum and to dance, both their own traditional dances and the dances they saw around them. For accompaniment, they clapped and drummed on anything handy.

A slave uprising in 1739 led to the prohibition of drums or instruments in the American South. But people could still dance. The beat of their feet on top of a barrel, a wooden sidewalk, or a table created its own music. People gathered at the end of the day and held informal dance competitions that sharpened skills and led to the invention of new steps.

After the Civil War, African-American dancers were among the first black entertainers to make it onto the American stage. They began adding metal "taps" to their shoes to enhance the sound. By the early 1900s, tap dancing had become a fixture in vaudeville, and soon it made its way into clubs and then into movies. From there, it became an established part of popular American culture.

1. **Recognizing Words in Context**

   Find the word *prohibition* in the passage. One definition below is a *synonym* for that word; it means the same or almost the same thing. One definition is an *antonym;* it has the opposite or nearly opposite meaning. The other has a completely different meaning. Label the definitions S for *synonym,* A for *antonym,* and D for *different.*

   _____ a. ban

   _____ b. development

   _____ c. encouragement

2. **Distinguishing Fact from Opinion**

   Two of the statements below present *facts,* which can be proved correct. The other statement is an *opinion,* which expresses someone's thoughts or beliefs. Label the statements F for *fact* and O for *opinion.*

   _____ a After the Civil War, African-American dancers were among the first black entertainers on the American stage.

   _____ b. Most African cultures included dance.

   _____ c. Tap dancing is entertaining to watch.

### 3. Keeping Events in Order

Label the statements below 1, 2, and 3 to show the order in which the events happened.

_____ a. Tap dancers appeared in the movies.

_____ b. People "drummed" with their feet.

_____ c. People added "taps" to their shoes to make the sound louder.

### 4. Making Correct Inferences

Two of the statements below are correct *inferences,* or reasonable guesses. They are based on information in the passage. The other statement is an incorrect, or faulty, inference. Label the statements C for *correct* inference and F for *faulty* inference.

_____ a. People in African cultures tap dance.

_____ b. Tap dancing represented a refusal to be silenced.

_____ c. Tap dancing relies on creating sound.

### 5. Understanding Main Ideas

One of the statements below expresses the main idea of the passage. One statement is too general, or too broad. The other explains only part of the passage; it is too narrow. Label the statements M for *main idea,* B for *too broad,* and N for *too narrow.*

_____ a. By the early 1900s, tap dancing had become a fixture in vaudeville and soon made its way into clubs and movies.

_____ b. Tap dancing developed out of African dance to include both movement and the sound of drumming with the feet.

_____ c. Tap dancing comes from Africa.

Correct Answers, Part A _____

Correct Answers, Part B _____

Total Correct Answers _____

# Answer Key

# Reading Rate Graph

# Comprehension Score Graph

# Comprehension Skills Profile Graph

# ANSWER KEY

| | | | | | | | | | | |
|---|---|---|---|---|---|---|---|---|---|---|
| **1A** | 1. a | 2. b | 3. c | 4. b | 5. a | 6. a | 7. a | 8. c | 9. a | 10. b |
| **1B** | 1. S, D, A | 2. F, O, F | 3. 3, 2, 1 | 4. C, F, C | 5. N, B, M | | | | | |
| **2A** | 1. b | 2. c | 3. a | 4. b | 5. c | 6. a | 7. b | 8. a | 9. b | 10. c |
| **2B** | 1. A, S, D | 2. F, O, F | 3. S, S, B | 4. F, C, C | 5. B, M, N | | | | | |
| **3A** | 1. c | 2. a | 3. b | 4. c | 5. b | 6. c | 7. c | 8. b | 9. a | 10. a |
| **3B** | 1. A, S, D | 2. F, F, O | 3. 3, 1, 2 | 4. C, F, C | 5. B, M, N | | | | | |
| **4A** | 1. b | 2. c | 3. b | 4. c | 5. c | 6. a | 7. b | 8. b | 9. b | 10. a |
| **4B** | 1. A, D, S | 2. F, F, O | 3. 3, 1, 2 | 4. F, C, C | 5. M, N, B | | | | | |
| **5A** | 1. c | 2. b | 3. a | 4. b | 5. b | 6. b | 7. c | 8. c | 9. c | 10. b |
| **5B** | 1. S, A, D | 2. O, F, F | 3. 2, 1, 3 | 4. C, F, C | 5. B, M, N | | | | | |
| **6A** | 1. c | 2. b | 3. c | 4. a | 5. a | 6. b | 7. a | 8. b | 9. c | 10. c |
| **6B** | 1. A, S, D | 2. F, F, O | 3. 1, 2, 3 | 4. C, C, F | 5. B, M, N | | | | | |
| **7A** | 1. b | 2. c | 3. a | 4. a | 5. b | 6. a | 7. b | 8. a | 9. a | 10. b |
| **7B** | 1. D, S, A | 2. F, O, F | 3. 2, 3, 1 | 4. C, F, C | 5. B, M, N | | | | | |
| **8A** | 1. b | 2. c | 3. c | 4. b | 5. c | 6. c | 7. b | 8. a | 9. a | 10. a |
| **8B** | 1. A, S, D | 2. F, F, O | 3. 2, 3, 1 | 4. C, F, C | 5. M, N, B | | | | | |
| **9A** | 1. c | 2. a | 3. c | 4. b | 5. a | 6. a | 7. b | 8. b | 9. a | 10. a |
| **9B** | 1. D, S, A | 2. F, O, F | 3. A, S, S | 4. F, C, C | 5. M, B, N | | | | | |
| **10A** | 1. c | 2. a | 3. b | 4. a | 5. c | 6. b | 7. a | 8. a | 9. b | 10. c |
| **10B** | 1. A, D, S | 2. O, F, F | 3. 2, 3, 1 | 4. C, C, F | 5. N, M, B | | | | | |
| **11A** | 1. b | 2. b | 3. a | 4. b | 5. a | 6. a | 7. b | 8. a | 9. c | 10. b |
| **11B** | 1. D, A, S | 2. F, F, O | 3. 3, 2, 1 | 4. C, F, C | 5. N, M, B | | | | | |
| **12A** | 1. c | 2. b | 3. c | 4. a | 5. a | 6. a | 7. b | 8. b | 9. b | 10. a |
| **12B** | 1. D, A, S | 2. F, F, O | 3. S, A, S | 4. C, F, C | 5. M, B, N | | | | | |
| **13A** | 1. a | 2. b | 3. b | 4. c | 5. b | 6. c | 7. c | 8. a | 9. a | 10. b |
| **13B** | 1. A, S, D | 2. O, F, F | 3. 3, 2, 1 | 4. F, C, C | 5. B, N, M | | | | | |

| 14A | 1. b | 2. c | 3. a | 4. b | 5. c | 6. b | 7. c | 8. b | 9. b | 10. b |
|-----|------|------|------|------|------|------|------|------|------|-------|
| 14B | 1. A, D, S | 2. F, O, F | | 3. 2, 3, 1 | | 4. C, C, F | | 5. N, B, M | | |
| 15A | 1. c | 2. a | 3. a | 4. a | 5. a | 6. c | 7. b | 8. b | 9. a | 10. a |
| 15B | 1. S, A, D | 2. O, F, F | | 3. 2, 1, 3 | | 4. F, C, C | | 5. B, N, M | | |
| 16A | 1. b | 2. c | 3. c | 4. c | 5. b | 6. a | 7. b | 8. c | 9. c | 10. a |
| 16B | 1. A, S, D | 2. F, F, O | | 3. 2, 3, 1 | | 4. C, F, C | | 5. B, M, N | | |
| 17A | 1. c | 2. a | 3. c | 4. a | 5. b | 6. c | 7. c | 8. b | 9. a | 10. a |
| 17B | 1. A, S, D | 2. F, F, O | | 3. 1, 2, 3 | | 4. C, F, C | | 5. M, N, B | | |
| 18A | 1. b | 2. b | 3. b | 4. b | 5. c | 6. b | 7. b | 8. b | 9. b | 10. a |
| 18B | 1. S, D, A | 2. O, F, F | | 3. 1, 2, 3 | | 4. C, F, C | | 5. N, B, M | | |
| 19A | 1. a | 2. b | 3. c | 4. a | 5. c | 6. b | 7. b | 8. a | 9. b | 10. a |
| 19B | 1. D, S, A | 2. F, F, O | | 3. 1, 2, 3 | | 4. C, F, C | | 5. B, N, M | | |
| 20A | 1. c | 2. c | 3. c | 4. b | 5. a | 6. c | 7. a | 8. c | 9. b | 10. b |
| 20B | 1. S, A, D | 2. F, O, F | | 3. 2, 1, 3 | | 4. C, C, F | | 5. M, B, N | | |
| 21A | 1. c | 2. a | 3. b | 4. a | 5. b | 6. c | 7. b | 8. b | 9. a | 10. a |
| 21B | 1. D, S, A | 2. F, F, O | | 3. 2, 3, 1 | | 4. C, F, C | | 5. B, N, M | | |
| 22A | 1. c | 2. b | 3. a | 4. b | 5. c | 6. b | 7. a | 8. a | 9. c | 10. b |
| 22B | 1. A, D, S | 2. O, F, F | | 3. 1, 3, 2 | | 4. F, C, C | | 5. B, M, N | | |
| 23A | 1. b | 2. b | 3. c | 4. c | 5. a | 6. b | 7. c | 8. c | 9. a | 10. a |
| 23B | 1. A, S, D | 2. F, O, F | | 3. 1, 3, 2 | | 4. C, C, F | | 5. N, B, M | | |
| 24A | 1. c | 2. b | 3. c | 4. a | 5. b | 6. a | 7. a | 8. b | 9. b | 10. a |
| 24B | 1. D, S, A | 2. F, O, F | | 3. 1, 3, 2 | | 4. C, F, C | | 5. B, N, M | | |
| 25A | 1. a | 2. b | 3. c | 4. b | 5. b | 6. b | 7. a | 8. b | 9. a | 10. c |
| 25B | 1. S, D, A | 2. F, F, O | | 3. 3, 1, 2 | | 4. F, C, C | | 5. N, M, B | | |

# READING RATE

Put an X on the line above each lesson number to show your reading time and words-per-minute rate for that unit.

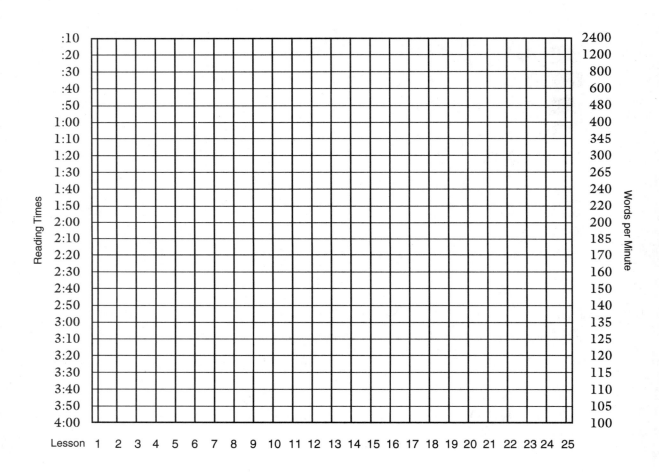

# COMPREHENSION SCORE

Put an X on the line above each lesson number to indicate your total correct answers and comprehension score for that unit.

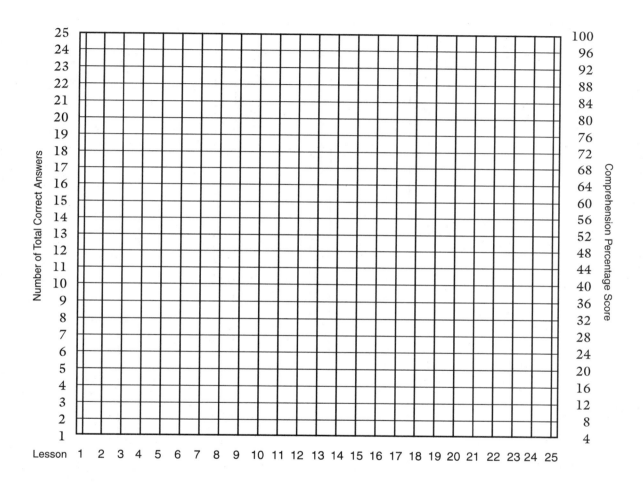

# COMPREHENSION SKILLS PROFILE

Put an X in the box above each question type to indicate an incorrect reponse to any part of that question.

| | Recognizing Words in Context | Distinguishing Fact from Opinion | Keeping Events in Order | Making Correct Inferences | Understanding Main Ideas |
|---|---|---|---|---|---|
| Lesson 1 | | | | | |
| 2 | | | | | |
| 3 | | | | | |
| 4 | | | | | |
| 5 | | | | | |
| 6 | | | | | |
| 7 | | | | | |
| 8 | | | | | |
| 9 | | | | | |
| 10 | | | | | |
| 11 | | | | | |
| 12 | | | | | |
| 13 | | | | | |
| 14 | | | | | |
| 15 | | | | | |
| 16 | | | | | |
| 17 | | | | | |
| 18 | | | | | |
| 19 | | | | | |
| 20 | | | | | |
| 21 | | | | | |
| 22 | | | | | |
| 23 | | | | | |
| 24 | | | | | |
| 25 | | | | | |